More Journeys through Britain with a Pack Pony

1988-1994

Jane Dotchin

More Journeys through Britain with a Pack Pony

1988 - 1994

by

Jane Dotchin

First published November 2022

by

Wagtail Press, Gairshield, Hexham
Northumberland
NE47 0HS

http://www.wagtailpress.uk

email: wagtailpress@yahoo.co.uk

© Jane Dotchin

No reproduction permitted of any part of this book without prior arrangement with the author.

ISBN 978-1-7397465-1-3

Cover photograph by J R Bracegirdle

CONTENTS

FOREWORD
Helene Mauchlen
Development Officer for Scotland, the British Horse Society

1	My companions; Sitka, Jester, Russet and Tinker	1
2	Journey to the New Forest 1988	10
3	Journey to the Scottish Borders 1989	26
4	Journey to Inverness-shire 1989	30
5	Journey to Ireland 1990	46
6	Journey to Hampshire 1991	68
7	Journey to Scotland 1992	81
8	Journey to Southern Ireland 1993	97
9	Journey to Wales 1994	122

FOREWORD

Jane Dotchin's third book is the perfect panacea for our hectic, immediate, and complex lives – it shines a light on the intrinsic goodness of the horse human relationship and brings us into an ethos that epitomises resilience, ease, fellow feeling and pure unbridled (sometimes literally!) joy.

Having had the pleasure of being Jane's friend for over a decade it is an honour to be asked to write this foreword, as meeting Jane and reading her books are a moral lesson to us all: she always pulls us up short. Her epic journeys in all four nations of the UK reflect on the work of the British Horse Society as she wrestles with access to the countryside, locked gates, obstacles, and traffic – all to be overcome by faith and determination.

From her wholesome low impact life led off grid as she milks her own cows and makes her own butter; to her lifelong riding adventures, Jane and her stories are so self-sufficient, humbling, yet trustful. Her upright Christian compass can keep us all right in our lives. Every day she starts by asking God for protection (for Diamond and Dinky too!) on her travels and it works. Such faith, such insight, instant connections with everyone who meets her; always wanting to engage. Never hurrying, always having time, while living in the moment with total acceptance. From time to time in life we meet a person who is a guru who can guide us back to better ways – Jane is one.

We need to be more Jane.

Helene Mauchlen
Development Officer for Scotland
British Horse Society

My companions; Sitka, Jester, Russet and Tinker

It was the 19th November 1987 by the time we got home from our journey into Devon.

Sitka looked fit and well but I knew it had to be his last journey as a pack pony. He was now twenty-one years old and had a large cancerous growth which was just beginning to cause him a bit of distress. The vet had warned me that he would probably have to end his days as a pack pony after this last trip. He had been with me since he was a six month old foal and had carried all my camping gear over various journeys for sixteen years. He had also carried Russet on journeys for eight years in a saddlebag I had made just big enough to carry a border terrier. Tinker had joined us on our trip to Devon having come to me as a young black and white Jack Russell puppy, but after over eight weeks away, it had become obvious she could only be a half Jack Russell. The other half had to be from a collie. She outgrew her saddlebag and had begun to look more like a small collie dog rather than a Jack Russell.

It was now Jester's turn to be my pack pony. He was going to be four years old in April and had grown slightly bigger than Sitka, his older brother, but although I had had him since he was a foal, he had an awful lot to learn to take over Sitka's place.

He had had a saddle on his back and had accepted having me on him. Next was to get him used to having saddlebags behind and in front of the saddle – also to learn to cope with being tethered on a long tethering rope so that when I camped, I could tether him near the tent on a long rope giving him a large enough area to graze yet not stray too far away.

He needed to learn how to avoid the rope getting tangled around his legs and how not to pull to escape which could cause a nasty rope burn. He did learn pretty quickly but it still took several months of being tied to a large log with me keeping a close eye on him in case he got badly wound up then panicked. Eventually, as he got more used to the rope and realised how to avoid getting caught up in it, I tethered him to a stake banged into the ground that wasn't going to move if he did get the rope around a leg. By then he had learned to stand and wait for me to unwind it.

Eventually, he realised that if he stood and banged his leg on the ground the rope would come off. Soon he got really skilled at manoeuvring to avoid the rope getting near his legs at all. We did have one setback when practising with the saddlebags on his back. I stupidly tried first with empty saddlebags on a windy day. I got off him to undo an awkward gate and led him through when suddenly there was a great blast of wind and the saddlebags blew up then flapped up and down. Before I could get the gate shut and back on him again, he shot off across the field – the saddlebags bouncing up and down and frightening him more the faster he went.

I stood by the gate helpless as he raced off to the far end of the field. Was he going to end up crashing into the fence or was he going to jump over it? No, he turned around and galloped back towards me and stopped at a skidding halt right in front of me and stood looking terrified ntil I got hold of him and he began to calm down and let me get back on him again.

Four months had passed since I had returned from Devon with Sitka, Russet and Tinker. That wretched growth on Sitka's sheath had grown and was really causing him distress. Now I had to make that awful decision to get the vet to put him out of his pain.

Finally, I managed to telephone the vet and Sitka ended his life on March 15th 1988 – a month before he was twenty-two years old. Russet and I went into his field and sat on the old log that I used to jump over on the old chap in his younger days and we both wept together. Later that evening, I led Jester into the field for the night.

Right from the day he came to me he had run out with his older brother. There were eighteen years between their ages, but right from the day they met there seemed to be a rapport between them. Whether it was an inner sense that enabled them to recognise they were related or not, I wouldn't know, but right from that first day they were left together, Sitka, eighteen years old and Jester a six month old foal, there was that bond between them.

Poor Jester; back in the field he looked around for Sitka, then he trotted right around and still no Sitka. Then he yelled and yelled desperate neighs. All through the night I could hear frantic calls. It took him about a week to get over his loss.

I continued with his pack pony education, then by the end of May, I decided we would try a short trip up to Dalbeattie to see Catherine who still had Udina, Jester and Sitka's mother – now well into her twenties. Tinker was now too big to fit into a saddlebag but she was young and energetic. She could walk. Russet could still ride in his saddlebag then get out and run when we were off the roads.

I had trained Tinker to walk in front of us and keep to the same side of the road all the time. The collie in her made her far more obedient than a Jack Russell terrier!! There was a mile or two of main roads we couldn't avoid, but I could put Tinker on a lead and walk holding Jester.

It was Monday June 6th when we set off, Russet and Tinker running through the West Dipton Wood ahead of us. Then when we came to the narrow road heading west, Russet decided he wanted to be lifted up into his saddlebag. Tinker happily walked proudly in front of Jester when a car came up behind us and overtook Jester, then swung in front of him and hit poor Tinker and knocked her right into the ditch! Fortunately it stopped and a lady got out most upset at what she had done. It was hard to tell how badly hurt Tinker was, but the driver of the car agreed to go ahead and telephone a friend of mine who came to collect Tinker and who agreed to take her to the vet in Hexham, and look after her until I came home.

Later that day I found a telephone box and telephoned Margot who had taken Tinker to the vet, to see how she was. The poor dog had several broken ribs and had to stay at the vet's overnight and be put on a drip.

That had to be the end of Tinker's days of travelling with a pack pony. She was far too big to travel in a saddlebag and the roads are not safe for a dog to walk along – even quiet roads we had been on, with Tinker only a few yards in front of Jester and keeping well into the side. The lady in the car must have been concentrating on passing Jester and hadn't noticed Tinker.

Russet was now twelve years old and quite happy to sit in his saddlebag. He would give a quiet grunting whine to ask to be taken down, but if he saw a rabbit to chase, he gave an excited baying noise and leapt into action out of my hands before I let his feet touch the ground.

I planned to visit a cousin who farmed near Brampton on our way, which meant having to cross the railway line at the level crossing at Milton. The barrier was up and there was no traffic on the road. I rode Jester towards the level crossing, but as soon as he saw the railway line he put on his brakes and I could NOT get him to step over it! I struggled to persuade him to go on over it, but no, he totally refused. Did he think it was a cattle grid? But he had never seen a cattle grid! Maybe seeing these metal railway lines had the same effect as seeing a cattle grid? Whatever the problem was I knew he had to go over because I wanted to get to the other side and I wasn't going to go another way round, as we could meet another level crossing on future travels, so he just had to learn to go over them.

I got off him and tried leading him but those brakes of his were jammed on firmly. I looked at Russet who was sitting in his saddlebag. He looked quite happy just sitting there and Jester looked determined not to attempt to go near those railway lines. I turned him around and walked away from the crossing, then walked back towards it, but no, that wasn't going to work.

I had seen two men walking up the road towards us when I turned Jester around with hope that he might head back and over the crossing. They must have seen him jam on his brakes and refuse to move. They quietly came up behind Jester, clasped their arms across behind his backside and heaved and over he went!

The rest of our journey to Catherine's went well. Jester was a bit nervous as we went into Dumfries where I tied him up whilst going to buy some provisions. Then going along the road to Loch foot, we met a tractor pulling a muck spreader with a mass of black polythene flapping from it. He very nearly had me off him as he did a huge leap up the bankside and landed between some trees and I got tangled in their branches!

The weather got very hot on our journey back home. We had no rain at all over the whole ten-day trip. My water-proofs remained wrapped up over the whole journey so nothing to get dry before being put away ready for the autumn.

Tinker had recovered well from her accident and had settled down very well with Margot who said she was welcome to stay anytime I went away again.

It was getting near the end of the school summer holidays, a very busy time for the riding school. The ponies were all getting fed up with a constant stream of children of all shapes and sizes riding on them. I had always insisted on all children who came to learn to ride, learning how to saddle up the pony they were going to have their riding lesson on.

I could understand why a lot of riding schools got their ponies and horses ready for their riders, as it took up a lot of time, and patience, even with the few ponies I had. The ponies also got frustrated and grumpy, especially when the girth of the saddle was being fastened. Getting the bridle on often caused problems, as did getting some of the riders mounted onto their ponies. Over the years there seemed to be heavier and heavier riders who had no spring in their legs to be able to get themselves up onto the saddle! As they struggled and heaved on the

saddle it upset the poor pony who would often turn around and have a quick nip at an unsuspecting bottom!
It could be very difficult trying to keep an eye on each pony to see that it wasn't going to take its frustration out on its rider!

After the school summer holidays, the ponies were always ready for a rest and I was looking forward to going off on my annual autumn journey. I had been planning where to go with Jester this autumn as soon as we returned from our visit to Catherine's in June. Although the traffic on the roads in the south was getting worse, the bridleways were improving. More and more of the bridleways which had become fenced off or overgrown and unusable, were being opened up. Scotland had rights of way but no bridleways one could rely on which were open for horses.

A school friend I had kept in touch with over the years had gone to live in the New Forest and suggested I ride down to see her. So, on Monday 5th September 1988, Jester, Russet and I set off for the New Forest.

2

Journey to the New Forest
1988

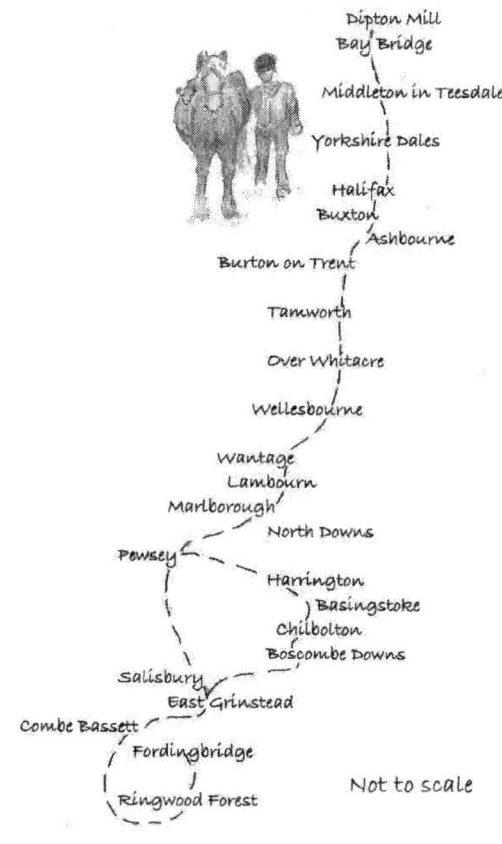

Dipton Mill
Bay Bridge
Middleton in Teesdale
Yorkshire Dales
Halifax
Buxton
Ashbourne
Burton on Trent
Tamworth
Over Whitacre
Wellesbourne
Wantage
Lambourn
Marlborough
North Downs
Pewsey
Harrington
Basingstoke
Chilbolton
Boscombe Downs
Salisbury
East Grinstead
Combe Bassett
Fordingbridge
Ringwood Forest

Not to scale

It was a miserable wet day but I could saddle up and get the saddlebags onto Jester in his stable then put the waterproof sheet over the top of everything before we set off in the rain. It was the first time Jester had had the large waterproof sheet on him. It had been so dry during our trip in June, I hadn't needed to use it, so it had remained rolled up and strapped behind the saddle with the tent. I threw it over his back in the stable. He did flinch a bit but once I had it tied down to the bottom of the saddlebags to keep it in place he accepted it and with my waterproof trousers on, I sat on top of it on Jester's back, and off we went!

The next day was cold but dry, so I wrapped up the waterproof sheet and strapped it in its place behind the tent on Jester's back. We got up by Tan Hill before going on to Hawes in the Yorkshire Dales, when the wind started to blow and then it rained so I got the waterproof sheet out to put over the saddle and saddlebags. As the wind caught the sheet it flapped madly. Jester really got alarmed but I had the reins held firmly with my arm through them and managed to hold him and get the sheet in place, then get back onto him.

We continued on towards Keld and found somewhere to camp, but the rain was still beating down. I got the tent off from behind the saddle and put it up, then got the saddlebags off Jester and into the tent along with the saddle. It was so cold and wet that I decided to strap the waterproof sheet back onto him before fastening him onto his tethering rope. It needed to be firmly on so it didn't slip out of place, but unfortunately, I hadn't got the strap around his chest tight enough, and as I undid it to adjust it, a sudden gust of wind caught it and it flew up into the air. Jester spun around and was off full gallop with the sheet flapping violently behind him and was away out of sight!!

Russet had decided it was too wet to stay outside so had crept into the tent. I set off in the direction Jester had gone realising I could have a long trek ahead of me. After a while I saw him in the distance. It looked as if he had come to a gate. I saw him turn around then come galloping back towards me. As he got nearer, I waved my arms in the air hoping he wouldn't gallop straight into me. He stopped, but I could see by the terrified look in his eyes, that if one puff of wind should move the sheet which was lying in a mangled muddy mess behind him, he would be off again. I quietly and cautiously bent down and got the one strap holding it onto him undone. What a relief!! I got it folded up and firmly under my left arm then led him back to the tent and put him on his tether. I then joined Russet, but had to leave Jester with no waterproof sheet on his back to keep him dry!

It took a long time for him to accept that waterproof sheet over his back. We had plenty of wet days for him to get used to it and I had to be extra careful when putting it on him to make sure, if there was any wind, that he was facing into it and that I got the fastening at the front fastened first.

We had been doing twenty or more miles a day. Jester was a strong sturdy Haflinger but he was only four years old. I didn't expect him to carry me, plus all the packs all those miles each day, so I was riding half the time and leading him half the time. He soon began to realise it was far easier walking up steep hills without me on his back, so as soon as we got to a steep hill, he stopped and waited for me to dismount, and then lead him.

Once we got south of Derbyshire where there were far less steep hills, he would stop as soon as even the slightest hill was ahead of him. It got a bit ridiculous. Sometimes I had only just got back onto him again after walking several miles and we would come to a short stretch of road or track going slightly uphill, and he would stop, hoping I would get off him again, but I could feel he wasn't really tired.

Russet had decided that now he was getting older he was really past chasing rabbits far. They went too fast for him. We were picnicking one day by an old tumbled down wall. Russet put up a rabbit in the long grass just behind Jester and it shot into a hole between the stones of the old wall. He forgot all about sharing my bread and cheese and spent all the time tugging at bits of soil and old grass around the hole, then poking his nose inside it and yapping with excitement. Whether the rabbit was cowering inside the wall or had shot out the other side, I wasn't sure, but Russet seemed sure it was in between those stones somewhere! Jester kept going over to have a look at Russet to see what all the fuss and excitement was about.

When we set off again, Russet refused to leave the hole in the wall. Jester and I walked on expecting him to catch us up. I was just beginning to wonder if we would have to go back to fetch him when a panting Russet arrived, came alongside me and gave me that look which I knew so well– which meant "I want to be in the saddlebag." He would look at me then look at Jester as he crouched down ready to be picked up. He then decided he was too tired to walk again that day and sat with his head nodding half asleep in his saddlebag.

We were down into Oxfordshire and into Hook Norton hoping to visit the lovely elderly couple who lived in the thatched cottage where Russet, Tinker and I had stayed on a very wet night coming back from Devon. "They are away on holiday in Austria" a neighbour told me after he had seen me knocking on the cottage door. "They'll be sorry to have missed you as they often talk about you."

We continued on to Swerford and camped in a farmer's yard with plenty of grass for Jester, but being Jester, he decided the grass on the other side of the gate looked better than in the yard. I woke up hearing strange noises, bangs, creaks and rattling sounds. I knew it couldn't be Jester wound up in his tether as he was loose in the yard. The noise continued and I thought I had better get up to see what was happening.

I crept out of the tent and shone the torch towards where the sound was coming from. There was Jester with his head through the gate, but he couldn't get it back between the wooden rails. He gave a whinny when he saw me. At least he wasn't panicking. I had to get hold of his head half way between his eyes and his nose and twist it round so his head was on one side then he managed to pull himself back, free of the gate.

Some days later we were getting into new territory when Russet and I had a night in a gypsy caravan belonging to a fellow who met us and stopped to tell me he travelled in his caravan pulled by a Clydesdale Horse. The caravan wasn't being used at the time so I was told I was welcome to spend the night in it and graze Jester in his field. He felt sure I would be better off hitching Jester to a similar type of caravan rather than carrying a tent and having to pitch it each night. I agreed how in wet weather it would be good not to have to pitch a tent then take it down, but pulling a caravan would mean having to keep to the roads. Bridleways were too narrow and the gates not wide enough for a caravan to get through.

The traffic on the roads seemed even worse than my last trip south a year earlier. Dual carriageways that cut right through the countryside in so many places, were the worst. And when crossing them it was nearly impossible to find a pause when both carriageways were free from traffic so that we could race across and not get caught in the middle with vehicles flying past in front and behind Jester. Memories of being stuck in the middle of that London to Brighton dual carriageway with Sitka and two terriers at Pyecombe some years back are never far away when I see a dual carriageway ahead. Jester wasn't as nervous in traffic as Sitka had been, but he had had a few frights by now with thoughtless drivers racing past him far too fast and far too close! I was beginning to feel him go tense whenever he heard the sound of a speeding engine coming behind or towards him.

After the night in the bow top caravan we got to a village near Whitchurch and a delightful couple with two Jack Russell terriers let me camp behind a farm building that had a clock tower with a thatched "hat" on it. A lovely sheltered spot but the clock chimed every hour with loud clangs. It did not seem to bother Russet or Jester but I found being woken up every hour a bit annoying.

We were heading towards Chilbolton on a horrible wet day. The wind got stronger and stronger and Jester was getting upset. The waterproof sheet covering the saddlebags kept vibrating as the wind got under it.

Even with me sitting on top of it, the wind kept catching the part of the sheet that was behind me and covering the rolled up tent across the back of the saddlebag. I had it tied to a crupper around Jester's tail but the wind got so strong the sheet still flapped up and down. We came to a dual carriageway – another one not marked on my map! Although it was a new map, it obviously had been printed before the construction of the dual carriageway. We got across, but with the wind and rain and speeding traffic on a wet road, I could feel Jester getting more and more agitated as we waited for a pause in the mass of rushing vehicles long enough for us to dare to cross over.

We continued on down a by-road with the roar of traffic behind us as well as the wind and rain. It was all a bit too much for Jester. He lurched forward as if something was about to attack him from behind, then suddenly he tripped and fell onto his knees! With the weight of all the packs and myself on him, as well as the way he was lurching forwards, he ended up skidding on his knees and skinning them both. A lady came out of a gate leading into a cottage a few yards down the road from where we were. She had seen Jester trip and fall onto his knees so had come up towards us to see if he was alright. She took one look at those poor bleeding knees then ushered us down to her cottage and into a paddock. She went and got all I needed to bathe Jester's knees then we plastered them with antiseptic ointment. She insisted I stayed the night there in her paddock, then we could see how Jester's knees were in the morning. I fully expected a lame pack pony with two swollen knees the next morning, but no, they were not swollen at all and did not look nearly as bad as they had the day before; so we continued slowly on. There were only a few miles to go until we got to our destination in the New Forest and Jester could rest there. I decided not to ride him and just lead him so that he would have less weight on those knees, as they must have hurt a bit.

We continued quietly on, along some good tracks. It was lovely being off-road for a while. Then there was a nasty bit of main road we could not avoid. As it was all open land with no fences, we went along the grass at the edge of the road. I kept seeing signs asking drivers to go slowly to avoid deer or New Forest ponies roaming onto the road. You would have thought they wanted to do the opposite and knock over and kill any animal straying onto the road, they were going so fast along the straight bit of main road.

Suddenly Jester stopped and snorted, his head right up and his nostrils flared ... then ... whoosh – he was off! He pulled the reins right out of my hands, snorting and flinging his head from side to side as if he expected something to be coming up behind him. I managed to come up behind him as he pranced on the spot for a while, snorting, then I looked behind to see what it could be he had seen or smelled, and there, with its head sticking out from some undergrowth between the trees, was a pig snuffling about eating ACORNS!

I'd been told pigs roamed in the New Forest to eat acorns as they are poisonous to the New Forest ponies. That was Jester's first encounter with a pig. He never forgot it! Even the slightest smell of a pig and he was ready to make a quick get-away.

I didn't see any more pigs during our time in the New Forest. Whether Jester really smelled some or imagined some whereabouts, I wasn't sure, but in spite of the damaged knees, he did a lot of prancing and snorting during our time in the New Forest.

We had some wet days as we set off again homeward. I wanted to see Stonehenge, so we made our way round by Fordingbridge and up by Wood Green then over towards Salisbury on some lovely tracks. Then I realised our route took us on a bridleway right alongside Salisbury Race Course – just as the last race was on so race horses thundered past us.

I did wonder if Jester would want to join them, so was getting myself ready to make sure I was in control – or hoped I would be in control if he sprawhich ng into action – but he didn't, he just looked in amazement and refused to move.

Russet was sitting in his saddlebag in front of me with his ears pricked, not sure what to think.

I heard the loudspeaker announce the winners of the race and wish everyone a good journey home. However, it was only then that I realised our homeward track joined the road where all the traffic was coming out of the race course car park! The sight of a pack pony with a terrier riding on it after watching race horses had most of the drivers slowing down to stare at us.

It was getting late and I didn't know where we were going to camp. There weren't many farms in sight, but I saw one marked on my map not far ahead of us ... I would try there. However, when we got there all I could see were derelict buildings and no house. Behind the buildings was a walled-in area with plenty of grass in it for a hungry pack pony, and room for a tent. Could I just go in there and camp? There was no-one about, no other place in sight and it was getting dark, so yes, we would stop there!

Next morning how glad I was we were in such a lovely sheltered place as the rain was lashing down and I could hear the wind in the trees round about making the branches crash and bang.

The rain did stop later in the morning but the wind didn't. We got to Wishford, then onto a bridleway that took us to Stonehenge. It was so windy and a sudden heavy shower beat down on us so we didn't spend much time looking at it, but continued on up to Larkhill on a bridleway. There were notices to say MOD territory but we continued on along the bridleway when suddenly we were stopped by MOD Police who said I couldn't go any further as there was an army exercise on. I got my map out to decide on an alternative route when there behind us were some huge army tanks looming up over the hill we had just come from. I got Jester off the track and we stood our distance watching the huge monsters lumbering past us with soldiers waving at us.

We went by east of Durrington and through to Figheldean then called at a house to check I was on the right track. A man came to the door and recognised me. I recognised him but could I remember where I had seen him before? It wasn't until he explained we had camped at his farm at Abington on our way to the New Forest that I remembered. He suggested I camped in a paddock by his house that night so I gratefully accepted his offer. Russet had an upset night as all through the night we could hear the boom boom boom of army guns going off.

The next day we got back onto MOD territory on the Old Marlborough Road. It was now just a track but I could see where the old mile-stones proved it had been the main road to Marlborough. This also helped to confirm I was on the right track. There were so many tracks, which were obviously made for the army vehicles we kept seeing.

We camped overnight on a farm just south of Marlborough. Next morning when I went to thank the farmer for the use of his paddock, he asked me which way I was planning to go next. When he heard I was going up via the main road as I could see no alternative route to get us to the next bridleway, he agreed and said "do be careful." He then went on to explain how bad the traffic was and that only a few days ago a horse had been killed on that road and the rider seriously hurt!

The traffic WAS bad! It wasn't the amount of traffic on the road, but the way people drove. There was one nasty blind bend which I imagined would be where the horse was hit and killed. Drivers overtook Jester without being able to see if anything was coming the other way. They were going at such a speed that if anything had been coming towards them, they couldn't have avoided hitting them. How glad I was to turn off that road! After that we had bridleways all the way to Lambourne.

By then I had run out of food for all three of us, so I was glad to be able to get all we needed at Lambourne. From there we were on bridleways all the way to Marcham. Some had been ploughed over making it difficult for Jester to walk on. The bridleways were often on the edge of ploughed fields and instead of leaving an unploughed strip for walkers and riders, the farmers had ploughed right over the tracks. The ground was wet from all the rain we had had, so walking on wet ploughed fields was a struggle for Jester. I got off him, thinking it would be easier without my weight and he wouldn't sink so far into the muddy ground, but I couldn't manage to lift my feet out of the wet ground quick enough to keep up with him, so ended up letting him carry me. He seemed to realise we were heading homeward and was not going to walk any slower. His knees had healed so well, even the hair was now growing back. He was also getting fitter and fitter after five weeks of travelling.

We were into Warwickshire where the M40 motorway was being built. The mud was awful as it had been so wet. It looked as if a flyover was going to be built at the place where the map said to cross over, and there were cranes and massive machines way below us down a steep bank. We had to slither down to where the unfinished surface of the motorway was, then get past all the construction traffic before clambering up the bank at the other side to get onto the bridleway!!

At first, Jester thought we should turn around and flee back the way we had come rather than face such an ordeal. Then when I insisted we didn't do that, he decided we should charge past all the terrifying obstacles as fast as we could. We did manage to get across more or less in control. The cranes towering overhead were the most frightening, but fortunately the drivers did stop them working as we pranced past and under them.

We were heading into Derbyshire and I had expected to tackle a busy road but I couldn't understand why it wasn't busy. Only two vehicles passed us, followed by a police car. Sure enough there had been an accident. A lorry had shed its load of canisters all over the road. We got to the "road closed" sign and asked a policeman what it was that had spilled out of the canisters. He told me it was human foetus going to a cosmetic factory. I shuddered as we passed.

After being on a quiet road, we ended up on a busy side road where all the main road traffic had been diverted. Being a narrower road with so many vehicles on it, was frightening enough, but then a huge wagon came thundering up behind us which made Jester go tense. Suddenly there was a loud bang. We lurched forward, but I managed to turn Jester around to avoid him bolting off ahead. There was this awful smell of burning rubber. The wagon had stopped which had slowed down all the other traffic. I could see the driver out on the road looking at one of the back wheels. A tyre had burst and I could see bits of rubber across the road.

Jester was still shaking with the shock of the bang. I slowly turned him around and we carefully continued on but Jester was continuously on edge. Every time a large vehicle came up behind him, I could feel the fear right through him.

We got to Wyaston before Ashbourne and called to see Maureen and John at their market garden. They had a caravan in a paddock where I had pitched my tent and grazed Sitka many times over the years. Maureen had seen me coming up the road, so came to meet us and led me to a new caravan. "Someone set fire to our old one" she explained . . . "all our horse's tack and lots of tools were ruined."

Two lovely kittens were playing by the caravan door. One saw Russet and fled, the other sat and stared wide eyed at him and wouldn't move. It was still staring at him as we left to continue on after chatting over a mug of tea.

A bleak cold wet trek up the Tissington trail next day after a peaceful quiet night at Thorpe.

Then it was back to my sister's place near Buxton for a few days' rest and a lovely hot bath to wash off all the sweat and mud from several weeks of travelling.

After a few days rest, Jester was full of energy when we set out on our last lap homeward. Even Russet was keen to be on the move again. When he saw me saddle up Jester, his barks of excitement had Jester and myself wanting to block our ears from the noise he made.

Once back into Derbyshire I always feel we are back north again, and nearly home, but so often it can be the most gruelling and toughest part at the end of a journey south.

The weather can change so suddenly and with a lot of high exposed ground to go over, it can be a challenge against wind and rain, yet in good weather it can be very beautiful. We set out in brilliant sunshine until we got to Diggle where the narrow canal goes through the hillside by the railway tunnel. Then we went up Boat Lane where the horses that used to pull the narrow boats after being unhitched, were led up over the hill to meet the boats again that had been pushed through the tunnel by men's legs up against the side walls.

As we climbed up the lane onto the bleak hillside over to Marsden, the weather changed to driving rain and a cold wind. We were glad to get to Taylor's farm and in the shelter of his cow shed, even though all the cows were inside, tied in stalls opposite us and there was the odd splatter of cow poo hitting us as it splashed off the concrete floor!!

We were heading for Gargrave in the Yorkshire Dales to go and visit Veronica, the lovely lady who always gave me a great welcome whenever I called to see her. Ever since that very first journey south with Sitka in 1973 when she saw me passing she insisted I stopped and both Sitka and I got fed and watered before we were allowed to continue on, I had to promise never to pass her house without stopping. We were nearly there when a donkey suddenly popped its head over a wall and Jester skidded to an abrupt halt, snorting at the sight of it!

It then gave a loud bray which nearly had Jester spinning around to run away from it, but I managed to stop him, so he stood there staring at it and each time it brayed, Jester snorted with his brakes firmly on. It took me a while to persuade him to pass it. We had a stop start jerky journey for a while as the donkey ran along the other side of the wall, popping its head over every so often to look at us – then braying!

After a dry night in a bed at Veronica's we headed on north into rain, sleet and wind. It was so cold at night that I slept with all my clothes on then had wet waterproofs to put on over them in the morning as they never got a chance to dry out during the day and had to lie in a soggy heap under the flysheet of the tent at night.

We only had two more days' journey left. The rain had stopped and the temperature had dropped dramatically before I got the tent up. Next morning everything was stiff with frost. Jester was scraping the ground, as ponies often do to clear the grass of frost before eating it, but he wasn't eating the grass. I got him ready and we set off, but I could feel he wasn't right. We stopped near Middleton in Teesdale for lunch. The sun came out but Jester wouldn't graze. All he wanted to do was to lie down and he was giving those tell-tale signs of kicking his stomach with his hind legs. Colic, but why? It must have been the frosted grass last night on an empty stomach when we stopped to camp. I led him on thinking if he wasn't right by the time we got to Middleton I would have to enquire about a vet coming to see him. We stopped in the village and I went into the Coop to buy some carrots. When I came back to where I had tied Jester up, he gave a whinny as I approached, then devoured the carrots. What a relief! He must have been feeling better if his appetite was back.

We continued on to a place I knew I could camp before going over the hill to Westgate. I decided to stop early, while the sun was still up, so that Jester could graze before there was any chance of the grass frosting over. It was early afternoon when we got there. I got the tent up while Jester grazed, then all three of us enjoyed the warm autumn sunshine for a few hours before the temperature dropped and the frost returned.

Thursday 3rd November. We were home again. The saddlebags with all my camping gear were piled into my chalet to wait to be cleaned, reproofed and various repairs that needed doing before being put away ready for next year.

Jester had a dry stable to go into that night and Russet had his cushion by the stove which burnt the wood we had collected over the summer to keep us both warm over the winter.

3

Journey to the Scottish Borders
1989

Jester and I were soon back into our winter routine with the other ponies back to riding lessons mainly at the weekends. Russet enjoyed his walks in the woods, but wasn't too keen if the weather was bad. Tinker came back from her stay at Margot's and was full of energy.

As soon as there were signs of spring and the days got longer, I decided to break Jester into harness. Osprey, the pony who had been doing all the work pulling the small cart, was now getting old. Jester was young and strong. He could pull the cart loaded with manure to spread, or when gathering in the hay.

I had been using him every day throughout the winter to carry hay in two old army kit bags slung over his back to feed the cows and he was well used to the saddlebags; so I put the harness on him and long reined him, then had him pulling a railway sleeper, but when I came to putting him between the shafts of the cart, he froze and wouldn't move. "Surely, eventually he would get use to it and move gradually … a little?" was what I kept thinking. I even tried with two pieces of wood as pretend shafts attached to him, but it was a no-win situation. If I had got cross with him and made him move, I could see he would have bolted off.

We continued practising pulling the railway sleeper, then when it came to the end of April and the curlews started flying overhead, I got the urge to get the saddlebags out and do the short trip up to Catherine's near Dalbeattie and stay a couple of days with her and see all her Haflingers and Norwegian ponies.

After the Spring Bank Holiday weekend at the end of May when the children had returned to school, Russet, Jester and I set off towards Dumfriesshire. We went the way we had the previous spring which meant we came to the same railway crossing where the two men pushed Jester over it. I wondered what he would do this time. He stopped, and snorted, then put his brakes on. I knew if I made a fuss and got him worked up he would just get those brakes so firmly on we could be stuck again. It would be unlikely those two young fellows would arrive again just at the right time, so I got off him and walked forwards looking straight ahead and he slowly followed taking great care to avoid the railway lines by stepping over them. Then just as we got to the other side the bleeps started and the barrier came down, thump, and we shot forwards! But we were over!!

On our way back we went by Langholm then over to Newcastleton then through the Kielder Forest. The weather was superb. It is such a lovely time of year, wild life is so active, days are long and in such good weather it can all seem so beautiful, it is easy to forget how awful it can be battling against wind and rain, then struggling to get a tent up and put all my things inside it without everything getting wet.

We camped one night up on the moors above Newcastleton. It was 10.15 pm by the time I got the tent up   Curlews, plovers, snipe and oystercatchers were still active as I got into my sleeping bag at 11.15 p.m.

Then I must have drifted off to sleep, but woke just as there was a glimmer of daylight. It was as if the curlews, plovers, oystercatchers and snipe had never stopped their chorus of sounds of spring echoing over the hillside throughout the night. It really would be the better time of year to do our long journey rather than the autumn but with it being a busy time of the year for the riding school and needing to see to my vegetable garden, then it would be hay time, I really needed to be at home and only away for a short journey then, leaving the longer trip until autumn.

Soon after our journey to Catherine's I needed to be thinking about cutting the grass on the hayfields. I got the harness out and onto Jester again and hitched him to the railway sleeper for a few practices then tried him between the shafts of the cart again. Not only did he go rigid, but he shook with fear. Instead, once the hay was cut and dry enough, I put it into pikes and then put a rope around each pike and hitched the traces to the rope and got him pulling the pikes across the field to the hay shed, then I forked the hay into the shed myself. That worked quite well. Jester stood as I attached the rope

to the traces then as soon as I said "go on" he shot into action – legs going all ways as I ran behind holding the reins trying to stop him from going too fast! It was as if he wanted to get the job over and done with as quickly as possible.

We had the usual busy school summer holidays with lots of riders and trekkers. It was Wednesday August 9th and I had just come back from taking some riders for a trek through the woods, when three students arrived – one leading a pony with saddlebags on it. They wanted to come and stay for a couple of nights. Could I let them graze the pony in one of my fields and let them stay in my chalet?! I explained that there was no room in my chalet for three extra people, but they could stay in the caravan I had across the fields by the cow shed. We put the pony in a paddock and I took the three of them up to the caravan. I then realised they had nothing with them to eat and only one of them had a few spare clothes in a saddlebag. She was the one who owned the pony and had come over from France with the pony to ride up into Scotland. The other two were student friends from Newcastle University she had met up with for the two nights.

Fortunately it was a fine couple of days and nights so both evenings I got a fire going outside and gave them a BBQ meal cooked over the fire. In between, they walked into Hexham and got themselves some provisions. Stephanie, the owner of the pony, explained to me the route she planned to take into Scotland. When I told her I was planning to go up to Inverness-shire in September and she could borrow my maps if she would post them back to me, she promised she would – and she did, with helpful notes by the inked in route she took showing me where she had come across locked gates, fences across tracks and dangerously boggy areas she had come to and had to turn back or had got through, but wouldn't attempt it again.

4

Journey to Inverness-shire 1989

It was 11th September, 1989 before I managed to set off on our trip to Inverness-shire. As soon as Russet saw the saddlebags out on my chalet floor so I could pack all I needed into them, he started to get excited. Then a few days later as I carried all outside ready to load onto Jester, he started to explode into his excited non-stop barking until we set off!

Up through the Kielder Forest, then on by Elsdon and to Alwinton and eventually on to Dere Street, the old Roman Road heading north. Then I joined the route Stephanie, the French lass, had marked on my maps for me and at Midlem a lady came rushing out of her bungalow when she saw me. She was so excited at seeing a pack pony and even more excited when she saw Russet sitting in his saddlebag. "I had a French girl with a pack pony staying with me not so long ago. She'd ridden up from

Plymouth," she explained. Then she asked if I would like to stay the night in her bungalow, but she eventually agreed to let me camp and stay in my tent. Russet and I went in to have supper with her, leaving Jester yelling over the fence as he didn't want me leaving him.

Russet loved going into peoples' houses. He always managed to persuade them, by his appealing look, to feed him, then he would find his way to the most comfortable chair to settle down on and no-one seemed to mind. Even in houses where it looked so clean and tidy and no dogs would be allowed on the chairs, they would look as I said "Russet, what are you doing up there on that chair?" and they would say "Oh leave him, he looks so comfortable!"

We continued to follow Stephanie's route and got to a farm at Cardrona Mains on the way to Peebles. They had had Stephanie staying there but had found it difficult having her just turn up and hope to stay with them, and graze her pony! Their horses had flu so they had to arrange to graze her horse at another farm so it didn't get infected by their horses – then they had to go and collect her and bring her back to stay with them!

The next day we went through Peebles, then up over the Pentland Hills on an old pack horse route but came to a kissing gate which is impossible to get a horse through. We ended up having to find a way round about which took us onto a busy main road in pouring ran beating at us in a gale. Vehicles were speeding past us on the wet road sending spray over us. Jester began to get nervous and he could feel me getting tense too as vehicles dashed past far too close which made him more nervous. A van nearly hit us which made us both frightened. I turned Jester up a side road and then we called at a farm, but couldn't find anyone to ask if we could camp. Then we tried another farm. Still no-one to ask if we could camp for the night. Eventually we came to a stud and livery stables and got a great welcome. Later, over supper in the house with the owners, they asked where I intended to go the next day. When I said I hoped to go over the Forth Bridge on the cycle lane, they explained that horses aren't allowed over the Bridge, but they would be glad to give Jester a lift in their horse trailer the next morning. We arranged a time for me to be ready to load up Jester into the trailer. I got all packed up in the morning in good time, tied Jester up to the fence beside my tent, when something gave him a fright and he leapt backwards, broke the fence and sent all the packs crashing to the ground.

Somehow I got everything sorted out and managed to tie two of the saddlebags together where the straps had broken, and led Jester into the trailer and off we went across the Forth Bridge and got dropped off on a side road near Dollar.

We spent a wild wet night in a straw shed near Auchterarder where the farmer moved some straw bales to give us room to camp. Then he came with hay for Jester as the wind and rain beat down on the shed roof.

We eventually made our way to Tummel Bridge then to Trinafour, across the A9 at Dalnacardoch and followed the track through Glen Tromie. I was now beginning to realise the vast difference between travelling north into Scotland and travelling south to southern England. Scotland had public rights of way and a lot of them were old drove roads but land owners could, and did, have padlocked gates across so many of them. Fortunately the keeper at Dalnacardoch arranged to unlock the gate onto the track after we crossed the A9 and he arranged with the keeper at Gaick Lodge about ten miles further on, to unlock another gate for me to get through, but I hadn't bargained on other hazards we met.

The track, to start with, was a good obvious landrover track. Then it changed to a single narrow footpath which seemed alright, but we came to a soft patch of ground and Jester suddenly sank into bog. I had to leap off him and let him heave himself out of it! I decided to then lead him as the track got narrower alongside a steep drop into a loch. With the hillside on our left and the drop into the loch on our right, I had to walk in front of Jester. Suddenly he stopped! I turned around to see that all the packs had slipped sideways. How was I going to get them back in place? There really wasn't room to unload everything and how could I avoid something falling down the steep bank into the loch? I tried creeping alongside Jester and heaving with my back to push the saddlebags up into place again, without falling over the narrow ledge and into the loch!! It was nearly impossible, but gradually the whole load got back into place after lots of huffing and puffing as well as swearing, as I struggled to muster enough strength to heave everything back into place.

We continued on alongside the loch then at the end of the loch the track was difficult to find. I could see it was meant to cross the river, but where? It looked as if it had got washed away in bad weather when the river had been swollen over the wintertime. I could see a good track on the other side, but there was a steep bank of soft peat that didn't look possible for a horse to climb up out of the river to get to it.

We walked up and down looking for the best place to attempt to cross. Once over the water Jester hesitated, then took a huge leap onto the far bank when the whole lot gave way and we both landed back into the water, but somehow he kept his balance and immediately made another leap and got to the top before more of the bank gave way behind him!!

Now we were on a good land rover track we would be alright, but we weren't. Next we came to a cattle grid. One of those very wide ones to stop deer jumping over. There was a high deer fence on each side and a huge six-foot high wooden side gate. I heaved and heaved to try to open it, but it would not budge! I heaved again and again, and gradually it did move, but to get it wide enough to get a pack pony through took a lot more heaving. Then the wretched thing needed heaving shut again once we were through.

We hadn't gone far when we came to another cattle grid with miles of deer fence on each side and another heavy wooden high sided gate. More heaving and we got through that one!

After that we came to another grid, but no huge side gate. This time it was a narrow little side gate, not nearly wide enough to get a pack pony through. I had to take all the packs off Jester, lead him through, then carry everything to where I had tied him up, and load everything back onto him again.

A mile or so further on we got to Killiehuntly Farm. It was getting late and we had had enough for one day! The lady at the farm wasn't too keen to let me camp but eventually she agreed "just for the night." I had to hope it wasn't pouring with rain next morning.

The next day we were going to Kingussie and got over the railway crossing without any trouble. I was looking for a place to tie up Jester so I could go to a shop and restock our food supplies, when a tourist bus stopped in front of us. The driver got out and came up to me. "I'm just off to collect a bus load of elderly ladies from the hotel who are on a bus trip to Scotland from Warwickshire and one old lady called Gladys was telling me all about a lady with a pack pony who carried a dog on the pony's back in a saddlebag. She said she had stopped at her cottage for a cup of tea last year. When I saw the dog in the saddlebag I wondered if you were the lady?" Yes, I knew Gladys who had given me a cup of tea over several years on trips south, passing her cottage.

We arranged to meet in the car park after he had collected all the ladies from the hotel, and to give Gladys a surprise. We didn't have to wait long when the bus arrived and stopped beside us! I could see faces peering out of the windows, then suddenly there was a cry of surprise as Gladys recognised us! They all staggered out of the bus as Gladys explained to them all how she knew me. Then cameras were clicking as they all wanted a picture of Russet in his saddlebag with Gladys standing beside him. Eventually, the bus driver had to usher them all back into the bus and it drove off with a mass of arms waving at us as it left.

We had left Stephanie's inked in route on my maps several days ago. She had headed west then gone south again. I wanted to go right on up north, towards Aviemore, then over the hill track from Lynwilg to join the Wade's Military Road to Slochd. I had made enquiries from various land owners who had assured me I could get along the track with a horse alright. We spent a beautiful sunny day going along the hill track with the fine weather making the wild Highland countryside look perfect. Then we came to a deer fence with a padlocked deer gate. There was no alternative but to turn back and trudge all those miles back again.

We had passed an empty cottage in a lovely grassy area by the river Dulnain. When we got back to it I realised it was a bothy, why not stay there and tether Jester on the grass alongside?

I unloaded everything off Jester into the bothy. There was a notice inside saying "Do not burn the furniture." Then I saw bits off the staircase and an old chair lying half burnt in the fireplace! On the floor were piles of rubbish left by past visitors using the bothy. I couldn't help but think about the different ways peoples' minds must work, or not work! Can there be any excuse for those past visitors leaving piles of empty tins and crisp packets as well as empty drink bottles strewn everywhere? What was their mentality – was it because they couldn't think beyond their having finished with them so why bother to carry them anymore? There certainly couldn't have been any thought about the inconvenience to others, that's for sure! Then to start pulling the furniture and fittings to pieces to use for a fire without going in search of timber outside. Must have been done by people with depraved minds.

Russet and I walked down to the river for water. As I walked back towards the Bothy with the sun still lighting up all the surrounding hills, and Jester grazing peacefully by the Bothy; it looked so beautiful – that is until I opened the Bothy door and saw that stinking pile of rubbish ahead of me again.

Next morning as it was getting light enough to see outside, I opened the door to check on Jester and there grazing near him was a group of red deer. Russet decided they shouldn't be there and gave a bark. They suddenly lifted their heads, looked towards us, then were away off into the distance, covering the ground with their graceful floating strides.

We trudged all the way back to Lynwilg. It was a beautiful morning and we were on a good track through lovely wild countryside, but I was annoyed at having to go all the way back, especially after having been assured by the gamekeeper of the estate, that I could get through.

I had had my maps out in the Bothy to try and decide whether I was going to try and find another route to continue going north, or to abandon the idea, but I could not decide what to do. We needed provisions. I had no dog food left for Russet and my food supply was getting low. There was still plenty of grass for Jester, but he really needed some oats to give him a boost for all the work he was doing carrying all the packs plus Russet and myself. When we got back to the road, we headed towards Aviemore.

What a contrast from the quiet track we had come along. Now we had a mass of vehicles rushing past us plus the roar of huge diesel trucks belching fumes at us.

Aviemore was crowded with people as well as traffic. A lady came over to me as I tied up Jester in as quiet a spot as I could find. She asked where I had come from and where I was heading. When she heard about the trouble I had had with locked gates and my trying to decide where to go next, she suggested heading east into Aberdeenshire. Then she showed me a route I could take using back roads and forest tracks she knew. She had ridden along part of the old railway track heading towards Aberdeen just recently. I hadn't even considered what I was going to do when we got towards Aberdeen I was so keen to get away from busy Aviemore with all its traffic! We had a lovely trek along forest tracks and quiet roads into Aberdeenshire. We were near a village called Tarland when a man came up to me and said "Are you camping?" He then suggested I camped on his farm. He was from the south of England and had decided to retire up north and start an organic farm. He had wanted to find somewhere on Orkney originally, then explained how he had ended up near Tarland instead. I told him I had some friends who had just moved from Cumberland to Orkney. "Well you can get a ferry from Aberdeen that takes livestock," he suggested. It wasn't until the next day, going along a forest track, that I began to mull over the idea of going to Orkney with Jester.

That night we got to Sunnyside Livery Stables not far from Aberdeen. A very friendly couple were interested in what I was doing. When I explained I had been thinking of getting the ferry to Orkney, they helped me contact the ferry company, then took me into Aberdeen to show me how I could get to the docks from the old railway line. I could ride the whole way along the railway line from their place right into the town.

It was early afternoon when we arrived. There were sheep being driven into pens down each side of the ferry's deck. We watched and waited, then a vehicle pulling what looked like a giant cage on wheels, drove up towards us and I was told to lead Jester into it. He walked in without any trouble, but when I walked out, leaving him tied up in the "cage" there were desperate yells of "don't leave me" as he was being towed onto the ferry. Russet had to go into a small cage below deck. I turned around to look back at him before walking away. He was sitting watching me, but didn't look at all upset.

It was an overnight sailing to Stromness. I had a very nice cabin with a comfortable bed and a basin with hot water so I could wash my hair! Because I was classed as a livestock haulier, I was told I could join all the other hauliers for a meal – a huge plateful of beef stew! After the meal I went down below deck to see Russet and was told he could join me in my cabin. So the two of us had a comfortable night, lulled to sleep by the movement of the boat.

It was 9.30 next morning when we got to Stromness and there were Barbara and Moira waiting for us with a large bag of carrots for Jester. The poor chap was desperate for something to eat. He had been in his "cage" from 4 pm until 9.30 the next morning without anything to eat. A long time for a horse to be without food.

We walked up the main Stromness to Kirkwall Road to Barbara's and Moira's cottage. More speeding traffic! It was as if everyone from Stromness was going to Kirkwall and all from Kirkwall going to Stromness, and all in such a hurry!

Barbara and Moira had a house full of dogs. I put Russet in their camper-van until evening, then joined him for the night. I woke up in the early hours having dreamed I was on the ferry, then realised I was in the camper-van being swayed by a gale blowing outside.

Our journey back to Stromness the next day was a battle against wind and rain. It was a different ferry this time, taking us to Durness. A very rusty, rattly "cage" was brought out to us and I was told to put Jester into it, then they would come out and collect him later. Poor Jester, he was horrified at the sight of it and refused to be led into it. I had to get onto him and ride him into it then I had to leap off and rush out to shut the rusty metal ramp behind him. Then we waited and waited until someone came to tow the trailer onto the ferry.

We got to Scrabster that evening after a very rough crossing. The men unloading the ferry seemed to be in a rush. They towed Jester in his "cage" out towards me at such a speed I could see he was beginning to panic. Then they pulled the ramp down and more or less chased the poor chap out, then slammed the ramp back up again and drove off in a rush. The "cage" rattling and banging really frightened Jester into an even worse panic. I had to wait and calm him down before I could get onto him. By then, it was late evening and we got to Scrabster House by Durness and a very friendly obliging young farmer let me camp in a paddock.

The next day, we hadn't gone far down a well-used track when we came to a locked gate, but I managed to lift it off its hinges, then heave and struggle to get it back on again! It made me realise we had to keep to roads if I wanted to avoid locked gates. Once past Dounreay, the massive blot on the landscape, we were able to turn onto single track roads and there was very little traffic.

Next day we wound our way through Forsinard after camping for a night down by a stream in a spot sheltered from the continuing gale that insisted on battering us.

Now we had side gates next to cattle grids across the road to contend with. Most seemed as if they hadn't been opened for years. One refused to open! It was so rusted and old that it was impossible to get it to move – so it had to be out with my hacksaw and saw through the wire fence next to it. Fortunately it wasn't a huge deer fence and with a bit of persuasion, I managed to fasten the cut wires together again!

It was now the beginning of October – the stag rutting season! We stopped one night by a derelict shooting lodge and camped in an overgrown paddock which looked as if it had once, long ago, been a garden.

A large stag came to inspect us. I was in the tent with Russet and heard this roar, so looked out and there he was, staring at Jester. After a few minutes he strutted away roaring short bursts of disapproval at having a horse on his territory.

As it got dark, I could hear a distant roar followed by a very near one. Gradually both roars seemed to be near, then crash – a clashing of antlers! It was a moonlight night and I could just see the two stags, heads down, antlers locked. Then they backed away from each other, roared at each other, then charged with heads down and - bang - antlers crashed together again!

Jester was a bit alarmed at first and Russet got off my sleeping bag to peer out of the tent, then decided he was too tired to be bothered and curled up again and went to sleep.

I kept dosing off then suddenly there would be another crashing sound of antlers. This went on all night. It was only as daylight came that all went quiet again.

Next day we went down Glen Loth. The sun came out. What a beautiful glen, but what a contrast when we got down to the main road. From quiet single-track roads with no traffic, we came to the A9 through Brora and on to Golspie with speeding drivers racing their vehicles so close to us when passing, it was awful, but I could see no alternative way to avoid it. Even if we tried to get off this main road and onto the verge, it was dangerous. There were broken bottles, cans and a variety of rubbish flapping in the wind. Not only was it dangerous for Jester to be stepping onto a glass bottle, but flapping rubbish would frighten him and make him jump towards the road which meant he could have been hit by a passing car. Whenever a speeding, rattling vehicle came up behind him, he would jump sideways onto the verge to get away from it. Every so often I would hear the clank as one of his shoes hit a glass bottle hidden in the grass, and I was reminded of when one of my previous ponies had stood on a bottle. It must have caught the edge of the bottle and the curve of the broken glass had cut into its heel. Blood had spurted out of the wound at an alarming rate!

We were able to turn off the main road and go round by Loch Buidhe then to Bonar Bridge. Some beautiful countryside and a fascinating coast line, but back onto the main road and no chance of admiring the scenery. All concentration had to be on avoiding speeding vehicles that seemed to treat us as if we shouldn't be on the road in their way. One driver even shouted out of his vehicle – "You shouldn't be on the road" in a very angry voice.

We were off the very busy A9 main road and onto a main road that was a bit quieter, but still had some dangerous speeding drivers along it. We were not far from Evanton when a lady offered me a caravan to stay in for the night and a paddock for Jester to graze in. She bred Highland ponies and had a horse trailer and very kindly offered to give Jester a lift in the trailer and take us across to the Black Isle next morning, so we didn't have to go onto the main road,

After we left the Black Isle the weather began to get colder and I could see snow on the hill tops. I managed to get permission to go through Dorback Lodge Estate to Tomintoul but because I had a dog with me, even in a saddlebag, the keeper wouldn't let me go down Glen Avon. We had to trudge down the road from Tomintoul. Then we met a farmer who showed me a track to avoid some of the road. He assured me I could get a horse along it, but once again we had to turn back. A fence went right across the track and I could see no way around it, so we had wasted a whole afternoon by the time we got back to the road.

When we got to Ballater the quickest way south would have been up Glen Muick and over to Glen Clova, but everyone I asked about whether I could get through to Clova with a horse without having to turn back because of locked gates, shook their heads and looked doubtful.

Finally, an elderly fellow came across to ask me where I was going. When I told him he said "they are shooting up over the top above Glen Muick – they will not want you going up there today!"! Again, I decided we had better stick to going on the roads, so we went around by Fettercairn and Edzell which added a lot of extra miles to our journey. The lady serving at the shop at Fettercairn gave me a large bag of misshapen carrots for Jester.

After getting the tent up that night and giving Jester some of the carrots, I left the bag too near the entrance to the tent. Jester must have smelled them and got his nose under the zip fastening, pushed against it, and undid it enough to reach the carrots. After that whenever we were camping and he wasn't on his tethering rope, he would push his nose under the zip to look for carrots! One evening when Russet was having his food, Jester's nose appeared under the zipped-up entrance to the tent. Russet was sure he was about to pinch his food and he gave Jester a sudden nip on the nose! Jester was a lot more cautious after that and Russet decided he would be on guard duty and not allow Jester anywhere near the entrance to the tent again!

The kind folks at the stud farm who had given us a lift in their horse trailer over the Forth Bridge had told me I was welcome to ring them to get a lift over, on my way back south again. From Edzell, we made our way on back roads as much as possible through by Murphly then Bankfoot keeping well away from Perth. We came to Dunning and then met them south of Muckart. Jester decided he wasn't going to go in their trailer this time. Fortunately they had brought a bucket with pony cubes which he eventually could not resist.

Seeing all the traffic as we drove onto the Forth Bridge, made me wonder at the strength of the construction suspended over the expanse of water holding the weight of all the mass of vehicles crossing over day after day!

The next day we got to West Linton and had some busy roads to face before we got to the Drove Road over to Peebles. It was now November. Days were getting short and the weather was getting cold as well as wet. I never seemed to have my waterproof jacket and trousers off for long. Each time the rain clouds cleared away and I took my waterproofs off, then black clouds would appear again and down came the rain. Part of me, especially my feet, were beginning to look forward to being home and having the luxury of getting warm and dry by my own fireside. My boots were worn and far from waterproof and my feet were suffering from depression with being constantly cold and wet. They cheered up at night in my sleeping bag until the next morning when I was back into wet socks and cold wet boots. Even admitting that a lot of the trekking time is a long hard slog against rough weather and frightening times journeying along roads with speeding vehicles going dangerously close as they passed us, a large part of me was feeling sad we were getting near home and this travelling, camping life with my horse and my dog would soon have to finish until the next year. It is those magical moments at the end of a long day's trekking when I'm lying in my tent with Russet curled up beside me, listening to Jester grazing peacefully nearby; the sound of owls hooting in the nearby trees; or just listening to the running water of a nearby stream; or peering out of the tent on a moonlight night watching a herd of red deer coming down off the hills to graze on the lowland grass overnight, then disappear up into the hills by daylight next morning; the crashing sounds of those two stags' antlers that continued on through the night when we camped in the grounds of the old derelict shooting lodge; simple things that make camping so worthwhile! Yet there were nights when I was grateful not to be out in the tent all night.

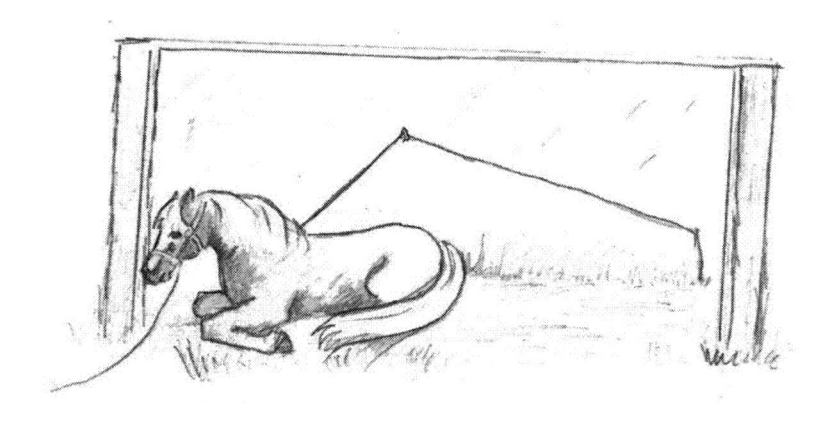

Coming from Peebles over the old Drove Road to Yarrow Ford it started to rain, then as we got higher up onto the Minch Moor the rain turned to sleet, then blizzarding snow! How glad I was when a farmer let me camp in an empty hayshed near Yarrow Ford. It had an earth floor so I could pitch the tent inside the hayshed and tether Jester so that he could graze on the grass round about the shed yet come inside beside the tent for shelter when he wanted to. He made the most of it by filling himself with grass then coming in to lie down in the dry on some old hay.

A few nights later, coming over the Cheviots on a cold wet day, Russet and I camped in a loft above a feed store in a lovely old stone barn. Jester had to brave the wet out in a field. Russet and I had just got ourselves setted in the loft when the farmer's wife arrived up the old wooden staircase with a tray with a pot of tea and some hot buttered scones. All the time the rain was beating down on the roof of the barn, it reminded me that it was no night to be camping outside. How grateful I was to be inside under a roof and not just a covering of proofed nylon!

By the time we got home the weather changed to beautiful autumn sunshine which made me wish our journeying hadn't come to an end after all!

Jester was pleased to be home. His pace increased the nearer we got. I think I would have had a very reluctant pack pony if we had continued on. My feet would not have been happy either! My boots couldn't have gone much further. The heels were worn away and the soles had become so thin, I could feel each stone I trod on.

Jester's shoes were worn thin too, and had become so smooth he kept slipping on the tarmac roads. The other ponies also needed to come in as the grass was no longer growing. They needed a daily supply of hay. It wasn't long before we were back into riding school routine with six fat unfit ponies and one very fit Jester. So, with seven ponies stabled and my few cows to look after as well as running the riding school, the short winter days were busy. By the end of January and into February as the daylight hours began to get longer, there was that lovely feeling again of "hooray" Spring is on the way!

5

Journey to Ireland
1990

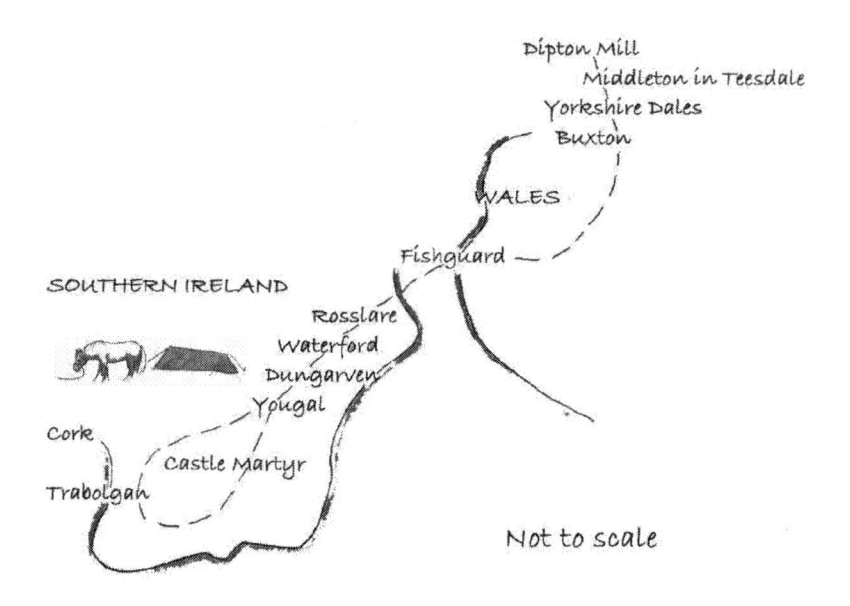

Map labels: Dipton Mill, Middleton in Teesdale, Yorkshire Dales, Buxton, Wales, Fishguard, Southern Ireland, Rosslare, Waterford, Dungarven, Yougal, Cork, Castle Martyr, Trabolgan. Not to scale.

I had got into a regular pattern now of trekking over to Dalbeattie each spring to stay with Catherine then o go on a longer trip in the Autumn. After the school Spring Bank Holiday week at the end of May 1990, Russet, Jester and I set out for Dumfriesshire and spent a weekend with Catherine; then came home ready to make hay as soon as there was a long enough dry spell before the busy school summer holidays. After the children went back to school at the beginning of September, I planned to go with Jester and Russet down to stay with my sister in

46

Derbyshire, then to go on through Wales and get on the ferry over to Ireland.

One of my past riding school customers over many years was getting married on September 8th and wanted me to go to her wedding reception after her marriage in the Registry Office in the morning. I turned all the other ponies out and got everything ready to set off with Jester and Russet next morning.

I left Jester to graze in the yard by the stables then got myself ready to go to the reception which really puzzled Russet. He had seen all was ready for another journey and was getting excited, yet I was making him stay in my chalet and going off without him.

Later that evening I got home to find Jester in the feed shed with his head in the hen corn bin.

It was hard to know how much he had eaten. There was not much left in the bin, but a lot scattered on the floor!

I dragged him away quickly. Hen corn is not good for a pony. Too much could make him seriously ill. I just had to hope he hadn't eaten too much! Later that night he seemed none the worse and the next morning he was fine, so I packed him up and off the three of us went – up over the Blanchland moors and towards Eastgate, then we climbed up over the top towards Westgate.

It was a lovely evening when we stopped, overlooking Weardale, so I decided to camp on an open grass area by some pine trees. Russet and I settled in the tent and Jester grazed peacefully on his tether beside us.

Suddenly in the middle of the night I woke hearing thumps and thuds beside the tent. I grabbed my glasses then a torch and went out to see what was happening. Jester was on the ground thrashing about then leaping up, then crashing to the ground again. My immediate thought was that the hen corn had given him colic after all. I watched him and eventually he got up and stood as if the worst was over, so I got back into the tent and lay listening. All seemed quiet and I must have dropped off to sleep.

As daylight came next morning, I peered out of the tent – thankfully, Jester was standing quietly and looked alright!

I got him ready and all the saddlebags onto him and off we set to go down towards Westgate. He was taking very short hobbly strides. I suspected the hen corn had given him a touch of laminitis and his feet were painful.

We hobbled on very slowly. I decided to try and get him to the nearest house down the hill as we entered Westgate to ask if I could use their telephone and ring for a vet to come and give Jester a painkilling injection and to help ease the inflammation in his feet if it was laminitis that was the problem. After a lot of telephoning from a very helpful lady, eventually a vet arrived. He gave Jester an injection which did ease the pain, but he told me on no account should I continue on, or serious damage could result to his feet. He had not to be moved for two days, then he needed to be rested for six weeks in a stable. Did that mean no journey to Ireland after all? That was awful!

Rita, the helpful lady from the house, became our saviour. She organised with the local farmer somewhere nearby for Jester to be put in a shed with a deep straw bed and for me to camp in a paddock alongside. Then she gave me a mug of tea while I tried to plan what to do next. She also gave me unlimited use of her telephone so I could do whatever arranging I could to get Jester home.

The vet told me to feed Jester on bran, so Rita organised a lift for me on the school bus to call at a riding stables at Alston Moor to get the bran. My thoughts that evening, while lying in the tent, were to maybe continue on with one of Jester's sisters I had bought from Catherine not long ago. Toscina was a good strong mare with a will of her own, and hadn't done anything other than riding school work on our own patch.

She would be a challenge as she had been when I broke her in but I decided to take it on. Thanks to Rita, I was back using her telephone to see if a friend would look after Jester for the six weeks he needed to be stabled and to ask if her husband could collect Jester with his horse box. In the end Rita organised with a local farmer who was taking some sheep to Hexham Auction Mart to give me a lift home then get Toscina in so I could take her in the horse box to collect Jester, swap the ponies over, then carry on from Westgate with Toscina.

All went according to plan and two days later I got all the packs onto Toscina and set off.

She stood quietly as I got everything onto her back. It was as if she was going to take to being a pack pony after all. Great!

We set off with Russet in his saddlebag beside me and got through Westgate, then climbed up over the hill towards Teesdale. Toscina had never been tethered before. I was going to have to be extra careful to see that she didn't get the rope wound around a leg and get rope burn. Then I could end up with another lame pony.

We got to Middleton in Teesdale. How was she going to cope with all the traffic? She seemed to accept it all; even a double decker bus didn't bother her. We got to Mickleton where two friendly elderly ladies let me camp and have Toscina loose in a paddock so she didn't have to cope with a tethering rope.

We had a peaceful night and I was feeling great! Russet and I were on our travels again after all. I knew Jester would be well cared for and Toscina was proving to be a good pack pony.

The next day we got into the Yorkshire Dales but by then Toscina was beginning to tire. She wasn't used to carrying so much weight or being ridden for so long. Again. I was able to camp in a paddock on a farm before Askrigg, so Toscina didn't need to be tethered.

Next day we set off in beautiful sunshine. We had a steep climb up over the hill ahead before dropping down into Askrigg so I decided to lead Toscina so she didn't have to carry me plus all the packs up the hill.

I was dragging a very reluctant tired horse, then suddenly she lurched forward, pulled the reins out of my hand and was off down the road ahead of me at a flat out gallop! On she went, away into the distance, shedding all the packs along the road as she went. I knew there was a cattle grid away ahead so felt sure she would stop when she got to it. But, no! She galloped straight over the top of it. I could hear the clatter of hooves against the iron bars as she sped over it! Then she was away out of sight.

All the saddlebags plus bits off the saddle and all my camping gear was scattered along the road. I walked along picking up bits of torn and broken things that had come out of the saddlebags, then the tattered torn saddlebags themselves. The tent had come out of its bag and must have been dragged along the road a while as it was torn with pieces missing from it.

Just as I was about to pick up the saddle and see what damage it had suffered, a van came alongside and the driver asked if I was alright? I explained what had happened so he said "jump in and I'll give you a lift down the road and see if we can find your horse." I put all I had collected in a pile by the roadside and off we went on and on down the road. Eventually there ahead of us was Toscina grazing by the roadside! She still had her bridle on, but nothing else.

I got out of the van, thanked the driver, then led Toscina back to where I had left the pile of things by the roadside, collecting bits and pieces on the road along the way.

With Toscina tied in a gateway, Russet and I sat on the grass as I sorted out all I could and decided how I could get everything sewn or tied together.

I sat for three hours sewing with the emergency sewing kit which had been thrown from a torn pocket on the saddlebag onto the roadside. The saddle itself was alright, but the girth was torn. I had to convert a stirrup strap into a girth with the broken girth sewn to it. With bits of twine, spare bootlaces, and lots of sewing, I managed to get everything holding together and onto Toscina.

Both the stirrups and the straps had come off the saddle. I found one in the ditch by the roadside, but no sign of the other one. I searched up and down the verges, then had a final look, but still no sign of it.

With the one stirrup strapped to the saddle on the nearside, so that I could get onto Toscina, we set off down the road and we got to Buckden that night. It wasn't until I got the tent up that I realized how badly it was torn, with large holes where the material had been worn away from being dragged along the tarmac road. Next day, we got to Kettlewell and called at a camping gear shop. They only sold tents to order, but with three tubes of strong glue we went on to Linton to camp. It was only lunch-time when we got there, but a beautiful fine day, so I got the tent up. I always carried spare nylon material and so I glued huge patches over all the holes and torn bits of the tent flysheet, then left it to dry all afternoon.

The next night we got to Oxenhope near Haworth and camped. It rained hard all night. I kept waiting for drips of wet to land on me, but not a drop of rain found its way inside my tent – my patching had worked – what a relief! We could continue on with a tent that was waterproof and so far all my stitching was holding.

We managed to get to my sister's place near Buxton and have a couple of days' rest before setting off again.

We needed to be at Swansea before the end of September if we were to get the ferry over to Cork. After that the ferry stopped running for the winter.

The roads got horribly busy as we got into Shropshire. I was in unknown territory now, no places where I knew I would be welcome to camp. It was getting a bit late and daylight was beginning to fade. I had called at a farm and asked if I could camp for the night, but got a grumpy reception, so continued on along a road that got frighteningly busy. There was no farm in sight. I was really getting worried as to whether we could survive as it got darker, as the rushing traffic with blinding headlights raced past us. Then as we passed a gateway to a cottage, a man called out "Do you want somewhere to camp?" He explained he was just taking his goat in for the night, so I was welcome to camp in the paddock for the night. It was a lovely sheltered spot next to the road, but at least we were off the road. It wasn't until next morning I realised the paddock was covered in goat "toddies." The ground sheet and the bottom of the saddlebags were covered in squashed goat "toddies" like squashed raisins stuck on them!

We eventually got into Wales, but it had taken me far longer to get there than planned. Toscina's plod, plodding walk was slower than Jester's pace and we had lost time changing over ponies, plus the time it took to do all the repairs after Toscina's bolting off down the road. I rang the ferry company at Swansea to confirm we would be there in a few days, but was told they would be finishing in four days time and the forecast was bad for the next few days, so it would be doubtful they would be able to take us. "You would be better going to Fishguard and getting the ferry over to Rosslare," I was told. Whoever answered the telephone when I rang up Fishguard docks was very helpful, but I soon realised it was not going to be as simple as going on the ferry to Orkney when I led Jester into that "cage" on wheels and he was towed onto the ferry. This time I had to hire a horse trailer with the right fittings on it to fix it to fittings on the ferry deck which was now a compulsory safety regulation. Then I needed to fill in a form I had to get from the Ministry of Agriculture's vet on arrival in Ireland, but first I needed a form to fill in before I could get the right one from the Ministry of Agriculture in Cardiff. It all seemed so complicated that I was beginning to wonder whether I could be bothered with all the formalities and just tour around Wales and forget about going over to Ireland.

I had been given the name and telephone number of a haulage contractor so decided to try ringing there before making any final decision. "No I am sorry, we are not a livestock haulier," came the reply after I had explained that I wanted to take a pony on the ferry to Ireland. Disappointed, I began putting the receiver down when a voice called out "wait!" I lifted it back up again – "Are you on holiday with a pack pony? All the way from Northumberland?" I don't think he believed me at first. There was a pause, then he said "ring me in the morning and ask for Martin and I'll see what I can do."

Next morning with a pocket full of pound coins to feed a hungry phone box, I rang Martin. "Yes, I'll take you in my daughter's horse trailer. Ring when you get nearer Fishguard and we'll arrange a meeting place and I'll pick you and your pony up."

I forgot to ask him about getting the various forms I needed, then suddenly remembered talking to a lady before we got to Wales. She had racehorses and told me she regularly took them over to Ireland but got her bloodstock agency to do all the arranging.

After a long session on the telephone to directory enquiries, I got the number of a local bloodstock agency, then I got the number of a local racehorse owner who took horses regularly over to Ireland. When I rang him he told me he would be able to give me the necessary forms if I could meet him in Presteigne next day.

I walked back from the telephone box to the farm where we were camping and the farmer's wife called to me to see how I had got on. When she heard I needed to go into Presteigne to meet the racehorse owner the next day, she offered to give me a lift in her car as she was planning to go there herself to collect something.

As we got nearer Fishguard, I rang Martin again and he arranged to meet me with his daughter's trailer at Crymych that afternoon. We got to the arranged meeting place in good time and waited and waited. Russet was fast asleep in his saddlebag. Toscina got restless and kept waking him up. Eventually Martin arrived with the horse trailer and this very large overweight fellow got out of the pickup and pulled down the ramp at the back of the trailer. Toscina gave one look and put on her brakes and refused to be led into the trailer. Then Martin got all his weight up behind her and with a huge shove, in she went! Russet and I got into the pickup and off we went.

Half an hour later we were back at Martin's place. Toscina was given a paddock to graze in. Russet and I were asked into the house where his wife had prepared a meal and insisted I joined them. Then I was told I could have a shower and a rest in their holiday cottage and Martin would take me to the docks in the morning to catch the 3 am ferry.

We needed to be there a couple of hours before the ferry sailed so it was just after midnight when Toscina had to be loaded into the trailer. This time Martin had a bucket of food ready for her so she walked straight in with her nose in the bucket.
Once down at the docks all the clattering and banging noises had Toscina shaking as we waited to go onto the ferry. We could feel the trailer and the pickup vibrating as she shook with fear. Once on the ferry, I left Russet lying on the saddle blanket in the back of the pickup and a sweaty Toscina still shaking and in the trailer, as Martin and I went up from the vehicle deck to the restaurant with all the wagon drivers, to be given a huge meal. Then I suddenly realised I had to share a cabin with Martin

for the rest of the night! We were due at Rosslare at 6.30 am. I suddenly woke and looked at my watch – 7 o'clock. I rushed up to the deck to see what was happening. We were still in the middle of the sea, no port in sight, but we weren't moving. Someone shouted "It's got a puncture!" Eventually there was an announcement, the ferry's engine had broken down.

As the time passed and nothing happened, people began to get impatient. One man attacked the poor lass at the information desk as if it was her fault the ferry had broken down.

As tempers grew, people paced up and down looking at their watches and the atmosphere got hotter, then an announcement came over the loudspeaker with an apology for what had happened and hopefully we would be on our way again soon – followed by another announcement saying everyone was invited to have a free breakfast while things were being put right. The atmosphere changed suddenly – whoosh! - everyone dived into the restaurant including me and Martin, and we all grabbed as much food as we could. I even put some bacon and sausage on a paper plate to take down to Russet later.

By the time everyone had stuffed themselves with breakfast, the atmosphere began to change again. Then as time went on, I could feel the frustration beginning to build up again, but the situation was saved by the thud of engines coming to life – we were off! Martin had arranged with Customs at Rosslare to get me through quickly so that he could take us out of town and drop us towards New Ross then have time to drive back and get the trailer on the ferry's return journey to Fishguard. Being several hours late, the ferry was going to go straight back, so we had to unload Toscina at the docks and I was left holding her beside a pile of saddlebags and camping gear as Martin drove back onto the ferry. I got everything onto Toscina and Russet into his saddlebag, much to the amazement of the dock workers who had never seen anything like it before.

We were just about to set off when the pickup and trailer arrived back beside us. The ferry was in such a rush to get back and make up for lost time, that it had already gone by the time Martin had left us and gone back to it. He would take us after all out of Rosslare and drop us off in a layby between Rosslare and New Ross.

That evening we camped in a paddock by a cottage. All seemed peaceful with Toscina enjoying some good grass, when a swarm of children arrived and kept tripping over the guy ropes as I tried to get the tent up. Eventually a lad arrived with a kitten which attracted all the children.

Russet and I got into the tent and I was just zipping up the entrance when I saw an old man staggering towards us. He smelled of alcohol and was obviously drunk!. He insisted I should go with him into the cottage for a whiskey. I could see he was going to join me in the tent if I didn't go with him, but I had no intention of having a whiskey!

As we walked towards the cottage, he kept tottering towards me and hanging onto me for support. What a relief it was as we got to the cottage, to find his grand-daughter was waiting to greet me and had a cup of tea ready.

As we tried to talk above the huge TV blasting forth Coronation Street, a toddler was crawling around amongst the chaos on the floor.

Eventually I was able to get back to the tent and avoid the old man's attempts to kiss me goodnight!

Next morning, I got Toscina packed up and we were just about ready to set off when she decided to try and bolt off. I had hold of the reins and managed to grab the gatepost for support and hang onto her as she spun round me bucking and kicking out. I was determined she was not going to charge off and leave everything torn and broken again. After a while she finally gave up and stood as if nothing had happened. I checked everything and had to do some quick emergency repairs where some straps had given way. It took me a while to adjust to Irish maps. They were difficult to follow and very much out of date.

It rained and the wind blew as we headed towards Waterford. Several times I called at houses to check where I was, or to ask about a track marked on the map, but everyone I asked insisted I join them for a cup of tea before I was able to continue on.

My plan was to go south to join some friends who were staying at a holiday camp for a Church Conference at Trabolgan on the coast east of Cork. I had no idea what to expect or where I would be able to camp and put Toscina.

"Trabolgan Holiday Village" – I could see the notice ahead of us, then as we got nearer, I read underneath the notice "No pets allowed!"! Oh dear, here I was with a horse and a dog!

As we got nearer still, a lady came towards me – "we have been expecting you and have made arrangements with the management for you to camp and graze your horse up the hillside beyond the holiday cottages." I took Toscina to where she directed me. What a beautiful spot! There was lots of grass for Toscina, plenty of room to put a tent up and the most beautiful view of the coast. The sun shone, all looked perfect, and we were well out of sight of all the holiday cottages, but how was I going to stop Toscina straying off down towards all the beautifully mown lawns below us; there was no fence at all. She was now learning to cope with the tethering rope. She realised that if she got wound up with the rope round her legs, just to stand and wait for me to rescue her. As I looked around, I could see nothing to tie the rope to. I eventually found a large lump of wood, tied the rope to it, then threw the wood into a clump of brambles. It worked well! Whenever she got wound up with the rope I could hear the rustling noise of the brambles as the wood moved, and then I would go and rescue her.

After a few days Toscina felt well rested and as we set off again, I could feel she was very much on her toes.

We had just left Trabolgan when she suddenly decided to do one of her bolts. Fortunately, I was on her as she set off down the road at full gallop. It took me a while to get her under control by tugging violently on the left rein to turn her into a gateway where we came to a sudden halt. Russet and I sighed with relief! We were still in one piece! Then I turned Toscina around to continue on.

"Oh dear, she is lame." She limped back towards the road. Now what!? Had she strained a leg muscle coming to such an abrupt halt in the gateway? I got off her and waited. She gradually put the front foot she was holding up, to the ground. I led her forward. She limped but was taking some weight on the foot, so we walked on and gradually she was taking more weight on the foot.

I found somewhere to camp early and let her rest the leg. We would see what she was like in the morning.

The cost of the ferry was bad enough – what if I had to box her all the way to Rosslare, then on the ferry and all the way home?

The next morning there was a very slight limp on the bad leg, so I led her along. We hadn't gone far when suddenly she tried to bolt off again. I managed to hang onto the reins determined not to let go. She pulled me over so I was lying on the grass verge still hanging onto the reins. Fortunately, I had the inside rein tighter so she swung round towards the hedge and came to a sudden halt as I lay hanging onto the reins.

"Right," I thought. "If you can try bolting with a sore leg, you can carry me and Russet and the packs." So I got on her and on we walked. I could feel a slight limp, but it was no worse after her bolt and as the day wore on, I could feel no limp at all.

After that she never tried to bolt off again during the whole of the rest of our trip!

I think if I hadn't managed to hold onto her and she had gone off again as she had that first time, she would have probably tried to do it again. But I was taking no chances. She had to carry me all the time. I wasn't going to risk leading her, however tired she felt.

I decided to abandon any plans of going further west, before returning to Rosslare. Instead, we made a small loop around then joined the route we came south on from Rosslare.

I needed to telephone Martin who was going to come over to collect us when I returned to get the ferry. Every telephone box I tried was out of order, so I decided the best thing to do was to call at someone's house and ask if I could use their telephone.

Not many houses appeared to have a telephone (no mobile phones back then). I could see electric cables going to houses, but no telephone wires. Eventually we came to a large old house standing on its own with telephone wires going towards it. I tied Toscina to the gatepost, then knocked on the door. A very old man answered, opening the door slowly and eyeing me very suspiciously. I explained that I needed to telephone someone in Wales about getting my pony over on the ferry from Rosslare, pointing to Toscina tied to the gatepost, but he still eyed me suspiciously. Then I got out some Irish pound coins and handed them to him. That did it! He led me into his house and to his telephone and I got through to Martin straight away.

We spent a night camping near Waterford with the moon so bright it even shone through the patches I had glued onto the torn parts of the tent, away back in Yorkshire. Next morning those patches got a good testing to see if they were still keeping the tent waterproof.

The rain was so heavy Russet and I decided to stay in the sleeping bag until it eased a bit. We had to move by lunch-time or we would not get to Rosslare in time the next day to meet Martin with the horse trailer. We got past New Ross as the rain poured down, and were fortunate to come upon an empty shed near the roadside and so we went in to shelter for a while.

It got darker and darker as the rain got heavier and heavier. I looked at my map. Could we get to Rosslare in time to meet Martin the next day if we spent the night in the shed? I decided as long as we made an early start, we could be there in time.

The next morning the rain was still pouring down, but I could get everything onto Toscina's back, and the waterproof sheet over while in the shed, which was a great help. We set off for Killinick and I got some bread and cheese at the shop for Russet and myself to eat while I let Toscina graze before we got to Rosslare.

We got to the harbour three hours early, with the rain still pouring down. I tried tying Toscina up then going to look for somewhere to shelter, but she wasn't going to let me out of sight without making an awful fuss. I didn't dare leave her in case the saddlebags all slipped sideways as she crashed about, so I had to stay with her. After an hour, I was feeling so cold and wet that I led Toscina to a small store shed I could see with its door open. There was just room for me to sit inside holding on to Toscina's reins as she stood outside.

Russet sat on my knee and we both shivered in the cold and damp, but at least we had a roof over us, while the rain beat down on Toscina. A man came to lock up the shed and got a surprise to see a horse, then Russet and me inside. I explained that I was waiting for a horse trailer to collect us and he kindly said he would come back later to lock up the shed.

How time dragged, but it wasn't too long after 7 pm when Martin arrived with the trailer and we were towed onto the ferry.

We got into Fishguard at 2 am. Martin drove us up to his house. Toscina went out into a paddock with a Jersey cow and then I went into the holiday cottage that Martin's wife had made ready for me.

We set off again the following day through Wales along the Gwaun Valley with no rain all day. By the evening we needed to look for somewhere to camp. Toscina was now able to be left on her tethering rope without me having to worry about her getting wound up in it. We came to a wide open grassed area. It looked an ideal place to tether a pony and put a tent up, but who do I ask if I can camp there? I could see a pile of rubbish further along the road and what looked like a derelict building, so continued on to see if there was a house nearby so I could ask whose land it was. I could see ducks and geese and a few hens about, so there had to be someone living nearby. We passed a pile of old cookers, fridges, TVs, and old sinks, bits of furniture and a variety of indescribable "yuk." Then dogs began to bark from inside the derelict building. They were frantically pounding at a door tied with string and some were leaping up at an old window held together with bits of twine. I could see an old tatty caravan behind this derelict building but it didn't look as if anyone could possibly be living at the place, apart from the dogs and poultry. Suddenly a figure appeared from behind the building – an elderly lady with a walking stick.

"Hello, your pony looks well packed up." I explained what I was doing and was looking for somewhere to camp, then pointed to the open land we had just passed.

"Yes, it's my land," she said, and that I was welcome to camp there. I asked her if she lived in the caravan.

"Oh no," she replied, "I prefer four solid walls," then pointed to the derelict building.

I could see it had a roof, but the walls had gaps where the stone had crumbled away. Bits of old rags and sacks were stuffed in various holes. It all looked very unsafe.

"Come this way," she said, and she led me back towards the land. "The gate is here," She opened it so we could go through but there was no fence on either side – just a few broken posts and old rusty wire lying on the ground.

"Is that your cow?" I asked her when I saw it in the distance.

"That's my Dexter bull, but he is on a tether," she explained.

Having kept Dexter bulls myself and knowing what vicious brutes they could be, I hoped he was on a good strong tethering chain. I walked over towards it and could see a metal stake in the ground with the chain attached to it. It looked safe! I tethered Toscina to a tree and got the tent up, then handed some money to my hostess which she gladly took, and we settled down for the night.

Next morning it was back to rain again. We set off and I stopped by the "four solid walls" and a figure appeared in a huge waterproof coat with holes in it.

"You are off early," she said, as I thanked her for the camping spot.

We were heading towards Rhayader. The rain had stopped, but a cold wind blew. I had got off Toscina to walk as the road went up a steep hill, to try and warm up. We came to an area that looked as if there had been some mining works. In between the heaps of stone and old rubble was a collection of old buses and broken down vans and what looked like a make-shift "tent" with a tarpaulin draped over a wooden frame. All around was rubbish and filth. Some youths were watching me from an old rusty bus; two more youths were wandering aimlessly about amongst the rubbish. I called out "hello," but got no response. From their grubby, aimless look, plus the state of the tatty accommodation and all the rubbish lying everywhere, the general chores of living, washing, cleaning, tidying and repairing etc. did not appear to occupy much of their time, so I suppose life must be a bit aimless.

Later the next day we left Wales going over the Kerry Way; a long distance bridleway with some fantastic views over lovely countryside and camped at Moat, just before Bishops Castle. Settled in my tent, I thought of those "four solid walls" and those rusty old buses. How nice it was to be in my tent!

After we had been through Kenley and past Much Wenlock, we had to skirt around Telford. I had worked out a route on minor roads, but the traffic was awful. All the roads seemed so busy with speeding vehicles. There was the occasional bridleway but much of the time we had to go along roads.

One farm we camped on was near the M6 motorway. The farmer explained how he had his land sliced in two by compulsory purchase for the construction of the motorway. Now he was about to lose yet more land because the motorway was going to be widened to six lanes to cope with the volume of traffic using it. He was considering giving up his farm as he was losing so much land it was making his farm too small to be able to work it properly and to make a decent living. Farming, he said was his life, but he was too old now to start again somewhere else.

Eventually we wound our way into Derbyshire and back to stay with my sister near Buxton.

By now October was rapidly drawing to a close, and daylight hours were getting shorter. We needed to be back home by the first weekend of November when I had arranged with all the riding school customers that they could start riding lessons again.

After a couple of days resting and washing at my sister's place, I led a very wet Toscina in from the field to get her ready to continue northwards. "Could you not wait another day?" my sister said as the rain poured down.

"No, I must go," I told her. "There are only ten days before the riding school opens again. At least I can pack up Toscina in your stable and get the waterproof sheet over her before we go out into the rain."

Russet refused to get out of his saddlebag under the waterproof sheet all day until we got to a farm overlooking Stalybridge and the never ending "concrete jungle" stretching away into the distance to our west.

A lady came to greet us. "I saw you heading south seven weeks ago. Where have you been?"

I explained I had been to Ireland and was on my way home, then asked if she could let me camp somewhere for the night.

"Camp in this weather!" she exclaimed, then called her husband.

"She wants to camp!"

"What about the stables over there?" he called back.

She then led me to an old shed and opened the door.

"You can go in there."

There were two small loose boxes. The one ahead was empty, but a strange grunting noise came from the other one on my right.

"Our boar is in there," she explained.

"He is a Vietnamese pot-bellied pig. They are very popular now. We breed them and people buy them as pets."

I put Toscina in the empty loose box and Russet and I made ourselves at home as best we could in the passage-way alongside. There was a sack of oats I had to move, so I could have enough room to lay out my ground sheet to lie on. With the oats sack by my feet and the saddlebags by my head, and Russet tucked into the side of my sleeping bag, we settled down to the sound of Toscina munching hay and rain beating down on the tin roof. It was very comfortable as there was a thick layer of straw on the floor, but at first I kept getting woken up by mice running along the edge of the ground sheet by my sleeping bag. They all seemed to be heading in the same direction, then after much scuffling about, ran back again.

Eventually I realised they were looking for the sack of oats, but because I had moved it, they couldn't find it in its usual place. I tried making a noise banging on the side of the partition between me and Toscina, but they didn't take much notice at all, and each time I banged, I got showered with dust and cobwebs, so decided to ignore them and I dozed off again. Suddenly there was this incredible noise – a bit like a "sick" motorbike engine. It came from the loose box next to Toscina. It stopped then started again. It came from where the Vietnamese boar was and after a while I realised it was snoring.

"If the mice can put up with that noise," I thought, "there is no way of frightening them with my banging on the partition - and not much chance of me sleeping for long either with those sudden outbursts of snoring from the Vietnamese pig throughout the night."

After plodding along in the rain all day, we had another dry night – this time in a cow byre.

After that the weather improved as we got through the North Yorkshire Dales, which all looked beautiful in the autumn sunshine.

We got back to Westgate and Toscina suddenly realised we were back to where she started from. She stopped at the gate into the paddock where I had saddled her up that day after she came in the trailer which collected her and took Jester back to recover from his laminitis. I wondered what she expected. Surely she couldn't think she was going to be collected and given a lift back home in the horse trailer. At first she refused to move, There was a very steep hill ahead of us so I got off her, but had to drag her up that hill! We got over the hill and were heading towards Bay Bridge when suddenly she decided to increase her pace and stepped out with such enthusiasm I couldn't walk fast enough to keep up with her. So I got back onto her and we got home in record time. When we arrived into the stable yard, she stood looking all around to see if she could see the other ponies. I put her in the paddock by my chalet and the good grass soon made her forget about the other ponies. I couldn't help looking at her: how fit and well she looked. Her journey as a pack pony hadn't done her any harm.

I piled all my camping things onto the floor in my chalet – they looked far from fit and well! The saddlebags had held together but I couldn't risk using them again on a long journey. The tent with all its patches stuck on it had kept the rain out, but the patches were beginning to peel off. I couldn't risk using it again. The pack saddle only had one stirrup and had baler twine slotted through a bit of old hosepipe I used as the other stirrup and a stitched together girth which really looked unsafe. Russet's saddlebag was beginning to give way and looked beyond repairing. It had carried him for fourteen autumn journeys and now that he rode more than running alongside, he really did need a new one for our next trip.

Jester had fully recovered from his lameness after gorging all that hen corn. Both he and Toscina and the rest of the ponies were back into riding school work over the winter.

As we got into 1991 and the days began to lengthen, I began to think of taking Jester up to stay a weekend with Catherine, near Dalbeattie.

By the end of April I had Russet's new saddlebag made out of some waterproof nylon material I had stored under the bed in my chalet. After a trip into Newcastle to a camping shop, I converted two new rucksacks into saddlebags to go behind the saddle.

Jester was fit and well, so after the school holiday week at the end of May, Russet, Jester and I set off to visit Catherine near Dalbeattie for a weekend.

Russet was now fifteen years old. He rode in his saddlebag most of the journey. As soon as we were off the road and onto a bridleway, he insisted on me lifting him down out of his saddlebag. If he got onto the scent of a rabbit he was off, full speed, but not far. He soon got tired and wanted to be back in his saddlebag. With his head resting on Jester's neck, he would try to sleep. On our return journey he decided he would just watch the rabbits from his saddlebag and bay with excitement but not bother to ask me to lift him down to chase them. After a few hours when I insisted he got out of the saddlebag to stretch his legs and have a pee, he was so stiff he struggled to get his legs moving.

As it got on towards September thoughts of how Russet would cope with another long autumn journey were worrying me. Would the old chap be upset if I went without him? Then wouldn't I be upset not having a terrier as a warm companion in the tent at nights?

Tinker was to go to her usual second home at Margot's house.

The couple who bought our old family home at Plover Hill where I had run the Riding School until 1984, kindly offered to look after Russet while I went with Jester down into Hampshire. Margot's son had given her a small dog he had got from a cat and dog shelter. After she had had it for a while, it produced a single puppy. As the puppy grew, she decided she really didn't want two dogs: would I like the Mum and she would keep the pup?

Piglet was a white Jack Russell sized dog but looked more like a whippet. Her only interest in life was to hunt dustbins and get inside them to see what she could find to eat. It only took her a day or two to sniff our neighbour's dustbins. She knew exactly when I took my eye off her and she would be gone in a split second, yet would be innocently back beside me as if she hadn't left me! It wasn't until I heard complaints from around about that neighbours were finding their dustbins tipped over and the contents scattered onto the ground, that I began to suspect what was happening. Then, one day, I caught sight of her sneaking off and followed her to a local dustbin and saw what she was doing.

It was most possibly her way of life as a stray before she got to the cat and dog shelter where Margot's son had got her from.

As searching for food was her purpose in life, I decided to always have a pocket full of dried dog food. Then on all our walks or treks, I had certain "muster spots" where she got a few pieces of food to eat. "Yum Yum spots" were how the children referred to them when we went for treks and had to stop to check Piglet was there at each muster point. It worked well and there was rarely ever a tipped over dustbin again in the area.

Russet settled down well back in our old home where he was brought up, and got on well with the new owners. Piglet soon learned how to make herself comfortable in a saddlebag. It took her a while to cope with her longer legs. They didn't seem to fold up so well as the shorter legged terriers did when sliding into their saddlebag.

6

Journey to Hampshire
1991

Hexham
Dipton Mill
Middleton in Teesdale
Yorkshire Dales
Hebden Bridge
Buxton
Ashbourne
Burton on Trent
Swadlincote
Tamworth
Nuneaton
Over Whitacre
Meriden
Coventry
Banbury
Whitney
Wantage
Lambourne
Hannington
Basingstoke
East Grinstead
Fording Bridge
Ringwood

Not to scale

We got down into Derbyshire and to my sister's place near Buxton in beautiful sunny weather which was a rare treat. Going through the Goyt Valley on a sunny Sunday was something I have never done over all the years of travelling that way. There were people everywhere! Some were true walkers dressed in hiking boots and shorts, but most had their cars parked all along the sides of the reservoir and hadn't walked far but were lying sunbathing. There was an awful lot of bare flesh looking red and burnt.

Piglet was running alongside Jester when a terrible smell reached my nose. She had rolled and was plastered in something revolting! I found a small stream but the water was running into the reservoir. If the "yuk" she had rolled in was what I suspected, I didn't want to wash her in the stream and the water then run into the reservoir, so I scooped up water in the camping pan to take it over to where I had Piglet tied up by her lead, then tipped the water over her... it took a lot of panfulls of water to get her clean and not smelling any more, and a few more panfulls just to make sure she was totally free from the "yuk!"

We only stayed with my sister for a couple of nights then continued on down the Tissington trail to Ashbourne, then to camp at John and Maureen's market garden at Wyaston.

They were threshing their home-grown corn when we arrived which reminded me of the days when we threshed the corn on my grandfather's farm years ago. No modern combine harvesters in those days! When the thresher came onto your farm, it was all neighbours helping to heave the sheaves of corn into the thresher.

We spent the evening chatting about Haflingers and how they used to be like Jester: square and sturdy but now were being bred to be more slender and higher and more as riding horses which is what most people wanted them for now. Their attractive chestnut colouring with flaxen mane and tails, has made them very popular.

We also discussed organic farming and how farmyard manure spread on the land helped stop the soil getting so dried out as it was getting over this period of such fine weather. Piglet and I had just got back to our tent when their neighbour decided to burn the long dead grass along his side of the fence opposite where I had my tent pitched. With all being so dry, flames and sparks flew up and over the fence. It only needed a hot spark to hit my new tent (that I had got to replace the patched one after Toscina's bolting episode on our way to Ireland) to melt a hole in the nylon flysheet. Was he doing it on purpose? Why set fire to anything outside when it was all so tinder-dry – and so late in the evening – and also right near my tent!! I had heard he was a bit of a difficult neighbour and not easy to get on with.

When I got out of the tent to check no sparks were falling on it, I got such a glowering look from him that I decided I had better not say anything and hope the tent would be alright. Fortunately, when I inspected it after the fire had died down, and I couldn't see him any more, I could find no damage.

We headed on south stopping to camp at the regular stopping places I had got to know over the years.

When we got to Bill's farm near Burton on Trent what a difference I noticed in him!

When I first camped there, he and his father were hard-working dairy farmers. Then his father had died and he found it difficult to cope with the dairy herd so had sold all the cows. Then he sold some land for building on, but on my last visit to his farm, I found a very depressed soul. The conversation over supper (which comprised of a thawed-out meal on a cardboard plate) was all about seeking a wife through an agency - then deciding what was the point of life and planning what to do with it?

Now the emptiness had been filled by a new hobby – renovating a 1920s tractor. I was led to a large barn and shown the dismantled tractor and all the carefully polished and painted bits spread out all over the barn floor. His whole attitude to life had changed – he had a purpose so life became more worthwhile.

We were getting into a busier area near Nuneaton, and we had the dual carriageway ahead which I knew we would have to cross to the other side to gain access to a disused road open to walkers and cyclists. I got Piglet into her saddlebag and got myself securely seated on Jester ready to make a dash for it, when I hoped there would be a pause long enough in the traffic.

We were all ready as I saw a lull in all the speeding vehicles, when suddenly – oh horrors! - there was a barrier right down the middle of the dual carriageway. What were we to do? If we turned left, we were going to get to even busier roads and into deeper trouble nearer Nuneaton. If we turned right and went along the wide verge, the traffic would be coming towards us, but we would have the slow lane of vehicles nearest to us, and it wasn't far to a roundabout where we could get onto a side road and away from the traffic. I decided we would turn right which was pretty awful, but what was even worse was negotiating the roundabout from the wrong side of the road.

Somehow we got across, but phew! It was frightening! Then we got onto a much quieter side road and soon we were back on the right route again. We had another dual carriageway near Merriden to cross. This time there was a gap in the barrier to get through. I made Jester charge forward when I saw a pause in the traffic, but when we got to the gap in the barrier, he wouldn't go through! It was narrow, but I hoped the saddlebags would be high enough on Jester to go over the barrier at each side of the narrow gap. Poor Jester, he knew exactly what width he needed to get through a gateway without hitting the saddlebags. This was a very narrow opening for walkers and cyclists. I had to get severe with the poor chap to make him go through or we were going to get stuck in between the carriageways with huge vehicles racing past us. We only just made it before a rush of speeding traffic came straight towards us then roared past behind us.

When we got to Merriden I tied Jester up and went into the shop to get provisions. The weather was still very hot and sunny so I had my shorts on. A lady was watching me tie up Jester then she came into the shop behind me. "Oh fancy riding in shorts" she exclaimed in a horsey voice with a definite air of disapproval! I turned to her and looked at her straight in the eye and said "I walk a lot of the time and lead my pony." She then became quite friendly and when she heard where I had come from and where I was going to, she offered me a stable for the night, but

I thanked her and explained I was going a bit further before stopping for the night.

Not many miles from Merriden we called to see Gladys, the little old lady I met in Scotland when she was on the bus trip. We chatted over a cup of tea all about that meeting as I hadn't seen her since then. She had a variety of photographs to show me before I left to continue on.

The M40 was now completed since we had crossed over amongst all the construction traffic a few years previously. There was now a bridge over it for walkers and riders. A little further south and we were back to good bridleways and off road a lot of the time. Piglet was getting into the way of chasing rabbits. It was obviously something she had never really done before I got her. Her sudden burst of speed was amazing, but she never tried to catch a rabbit. Sometimes she would end up overtaking one, then it would dart off in another direction leaving Piglet wondering where I had gone.

We were into Oxfordshire and had been camping outside a small village. It was another beautiful sunny morning. I had Jester packed up ready to set off and turned around to look for Piglet, who was usually sitting waiting for me to tell her when I was ready to go, but there was no sign of her. I called and called, but still no Piglet. Had she gone back towards the village to the cottage where we had been asked in for supper last night?

Jester and I trudged back towards the village. I noticed a dustbin lying on its side, then as we walked on, another dustbin on its side, and a mass of rubbish scattered on the ground, then another and there sticking out of it was a white tail! I yelled "Piglet" but she took no notice. Her head was well into the contents of the bin. She seemed to have gone right back to her days as a stray living on what she could find in bins. I got behind her and yelled loudly "PIGLET," and she came out of the dustbin, gave me a strange look, then appeared to suddenly realise who I was and started wagging her tail! After that, as soon as we were anywhere near a built up area, where there would be dustbins about, I made sure she was either in her saddlebag, or on a lead.

We were east of Wantage and heading towards Lambourne. The bridleways in that area of the downs are fantastic. Beautiful grass tracks for miles. I did have to get the waterproofs out one day when it rained, but that was the first time they had been unwrapped and used since we had left home.

The downs around Lambourne are a great exercise place for many racehorses which are bred and trained in the area. We did cause a problem for these stable lads exercising those horses. They had never seen a pony laden with packs on its back before. As we got towards Lambourne and I lifted Piglet up into her saddlebag, it made the sight of us even more scary. We had racehorses spinning around at the sight of us and bolting off away from me with the stable lads swearing and struggling to get control of them.

I kept stopping Jester and we would stand off the track hoping that the riders could get their horses past us. Many a time the horses would come towards us, ears pricked, then as they got nearer and looked as if they would pass us – whoosh! ...they would spin around and try to make a bolt for it again!

I had arranged to go and visit a friend who lived in Harrington, near Basingstoke, at the beginning of October, but planned to go on south first to where I had arranged to camp and graze Jester for a few days near Ringwood so I could get a bus into Bournemouth and attend a Church Bible Study Conference.

We got to Fordingbridge when outside a farm I saw a notice saying "horse and pony feed for sale." Jester's oats bag was empty, so I rode into the farmyard, past paddocks and fields full of ponies and horses. The yard was full of children and parents and ponies. We were soon surrounded by folk fascinated by the sight of us, especially with Piglet in her saddlebag. Then one of the parents went off to find the owner and tell him I had called to buy some oats. When he heard where I was going, he said he would telephone the farm where I had planned to camp and ask him to unlock a gate from the forest so I could get there without having to go onto the main road.

He handed me Jester's oats bag filled as full as he could get it, and gave me several free sample packets of various brands of horse feed to take as well.

We got to the forest gate just as someone was unlocking it for us. There ahead of us was a weird looking construction with revolving cylinder-like things with a slice taken out of each side of them. They were rotating round and round making a strange jangling sound. Jester stood rigid staring at it. We were going to have to go past it. There was no alternative other than going back through the forest and along by the main road. I tried to urge him on, but he wouldn't move. "It's a wind turbine," the man who opened the gate told me. I explained I had never seen one like that before, as I tried again to urge Jester on. I managed to get a bit nearer to it and hoped I could stop Jester from spinning around and fleeing from it, when suddenly he decided if he couldn't flee back from it he would make a bolt past it as quickly as he could. A sudden whoosh …. and we were well past it!

Jester had a few days rest as I struggled to adapt to travelling on a bus; then being in a busy town and then coping with sitting in a hot stuffy hall. It was just as well the conference gave good stimulating food for thought which kept me alert and not falling asleep . . . well not too often!

Tuesday October 1st. We were all ready to set off north again. Jester was well rested. I feared he might be a bit too well rested as having been doing about twenty miles a day, he was really fit. Then a few days just grazing in a field – would he explode with stored up energy? We had that strange wind turbine construction to pass on the way back to the forest gate. To my surprise, although he pranced and snorted at it, we didn't pass it as quickly as on our way to our camping spot!

We got to East Grinstead that night and ended up camping on the village green. I could not find a farmhouse with a farmer living in it! There were many houses named "something" Farm, with farm buildings round about, but they appeared to have been sold off to new country folk commuters who seemed to like keeping the name "farm" – perhaps it sounds genuinely more countrified.

I could only find one house alongside the village green with anyone in to ask if they minded me camping there for the night. By the time I got the tent up and Jester tethered, I had a variety of villagers coming to ask me if they could provide me with anything I needed.

Next day as we passed a farm a huge Alsatian dog came charging at us. I thought it was going to attack Piglet. Then suddenly I noticed it wasn't Piglet it was going to attack, but Jester. Then a lady from the door of the farmhouse shouted "It's alright, but mind he doesn't jump on your pony as he just wants to play." It seemed like far from play to me as it showed its teeth and snarled at us, leaping up behind Jester. I had to hang onto the reins as he got more and more frightened – then suddenly, the great beast decided to obey its mistress's call and ran back to the farmhouse.

We went on bridleways via Chilbolton to Newton Stacey and called at a farmhouse to see if I could camp, but it was another case of the farmer not living in the farmhouse. This time the lady at the house rang the farmer for me and he explained where I could camp in a field at Barton Stacey, the next village. The field was next to the church and the bell ringers were having a long evening practising ringing the church bells!

We were just a few miles from Hannington when a hare shot up from the long grass alongside the bridleway and was across the fields with Piglet racing after it. Both were gone away out of sight. I continued on with Jester, thinking Piglet would soon be back and catch us up, but no she didn't. We stopped and waited, but still no sign of Piglet. I turned Jester around to go back to where she put up the hare. Hares don't usually go far, but circle around back to their own territory, so I waited, and waited. It was getting dark and had begun to rain. They would be waiting for me at Hannington so I thought I had better continue on and hope Piglet would catch me up.

I got there but not a sign of Piglet. We decided we had better ring the local police station and see if someone had handed her in there. "Yes, we have a dog just brought in and it has a Hexham telephone number on its collar." My host drove me to Basingstoke police station to collect her. It sounded as if she had got lost, then turned back to her dustbin hunting days as she had been picked up by someone in a nearby village while on the scavenge. She was really pleased to see me. She never went far from me again all the way home. Partly I think because the weather changed and we had a lot of rain and Piglet really hated getting wet. As soon as the rain started, or if the grass was very wet, she wanted to be in her saddlebag.

From Hannington we were able to keep mostly to bridleways and back onto our route south.

After all the lovely dry weather coming south, we seemed to be battling against wind and rain most of our way home. There were nights when it was hard to pitch a tent, the wind and rain trying to make it as difficult as possible. There were several nights I was able to camp in hay sheds, cow sheds, and lofts. Then I had a good dry out and a bed at Buxton in my sister's house.

By the time we got to the Yorkshire Dales there was snow on the hilltops. It was difficult to find enough grass for Jester. After the dry summer, a lot had burnt off or not grown much at all. Then all the wet made the bare ground muddy and my feet were getting depressed again – in wet cold boots! Piglet decided riding in the saddlebag covered by Jester's waterproof sheet was the best place to be when she wasn't in the tent. She was really pleased to get home and be by the fireside, but as soon as Russet returned from Plover Hill, we made sure he got the best seat by the fire.

Jester and I were soon back into our winter routine. Jester joined the other ponies taking children for riding lessons. As all the ponies were now stabled for the winter, I spent a lot of time carrying hay from the hay shed to fill up ponies' hay racks and across to the cow shed to feed the cows. Then even more time was spent mucking out all the stables and the cow shed each day. Tinker, Piglet and Russet needed their daily walks in the woods, but as the track across the fields to the woods got wetter and the mud got deeper, Russet began to refuse to follow us and so I started picking him up and carrying him until we got to the gate into the woods, then he would run off ahead full of enthusiasm. Once he realised he could get a lift across the fields, he just sat in the yard and waited for me to pick him up.

By the time we got to the woods my arms were aching, so one day I put some hay in the bottom of the wheelbarrow, plonked him on the top of the hay and wheeled him across the fields, left the wheelbarrow by the gate into the woods, lifted him out, and off he ran. That became our routine start for our walks each day over the winter.

We were soon into February 1992 and there was a lovely dry spring-like spell of weather, so Jester and I started our wood collecting ready for the next winter. I had a couple of ex-army kit bags sewn together that slung across his back over the saddlebag.

Then, leading him and carrying a saw, we went into the woods, where I collected dead timber and sawed it into lengths to put in the kit bags to carry back to the woodshed.

In March we had a spell of very cold and frosty weather, followed by snow, then rain. Russet was very reluctant to leave his bed. I had to carry him outside to relieve himself. He would sit on the hay in the wheelbarrow to go across the fields, but when we got to the woods and I lifted him out, he would only sit and look miserable. He had been having difficulty eating his food and had lost weight, so I decided to take him to the vets.

"How old is he?" the vet asked.

"Coming up seventeen," I replied.

"He has done very well, but his teeth are rotten and I think he is in a lot of pain. We could pull them out but at his age, and from the condition of his heart, I wouldn't recommend it."

So on April, 7th 1992, Russet peacefully ended his days.

The place was not the same without Russet about – how I missed him!! We were into the time of year when daylight hours were longer and the riding school got a lot busier, so it was mainly in the evenings when going inside my chalet with no Russet to greet me I missed him.
After the school Spring Bank Holiday week, I planned to make time to do the short journey over to Dalbeattie to stay with Catherine Hanbury for a weekend.
Tinker went to her second home with Margot, and Piglet and I set off with Jester. The children had all gone back to school on the Monday. We got to Catherine's on the Friday - left on the following Monday and got home on Friday.
Now we were well into June and I was hoping for some good fine weather to make hay before the school summer holidays started and the riding school got even busier with riding lessons at weekends. Then during the week, children came for a day's riding bringing their own lunch to cook on an open fire which we had in a paddock beside the stream. Most children brought sausages which they cooked (or burnt!) over the fire on wire sausage sticks as Piglet sat and watched, waiting for someone to drop their sausage in the ashes by the fire. She devoured many a casualty sausage over the summer holidays and it didn't seem to bother her how hot they were, or if they were covered in ash. It was grab and gulp down as quickly as possible ready to catch the next one that fell.

On the last Friday of the summer school holidays, instead of sausages most of the day riders brought pot noodles in a plastic pot that only needed boiling water poured into them, then the noodle mixture swelled up ready to be eaten.
I put the old kettle on the fire to boil up some water; poured the water into their plastic "pots" as Piglet sat watching me. I did notice that none of the children had finished the contents of those pots. They were in too much of a hurry to go and play in the stream. I followed them down to the edge of the water as they jumped in with yells – "oh it's cold!"

Eventually it was time to get ready to ride again, so I called to the children to come and gather up their picnic things. "Oh" remarked one child, "someone has eaten the rest of my pot noodle." As they all gathered up their things each found an empty well licked out pot noodle plastic pot! Then one child shouted "look at Piglet" and they all began to laugh when they saw Piglet with a tomato sauce stain right round her head above her eyes.

Next day an uncomfortable Piglet asked to go outside very early in the morning and spent the rest of that day looking very unhappy. She wouldn't even eat her food.

When she still wasn't well on the Sunday, I began to worry as we were meant to be setting off on a journey north with Jester the following morning.

Tinker had already gone to stay with Margot. The saddlebags were all ready, but was Piglet going to be alright? Maybe it wasn't just the pot noodles that had upset her. Later that Sunday evening she suddenly decided she was hungry, ate her food and began to look her happy normal self again.

7

Journey to Scotland 1992

Monday September 7th 1992. All those last minute things that needed seeing to before we left to head north took up a lot more time than I thought they would. We ended up making a far later start than I had intended, but we managed to get to our first camping spot at Greencarts Farm just before dark.

Next night was at Tarset Hall Farm beyond Bellingham. From there we went on to Falstone then joined the bridleway through the Kielder Forest, stopping at Gowanburn just before Kielder Village where Piglet and I stayed in Janet Scott's caravan while Jester grazed in her paddock.

Janet knew my late Aunt Belle who lived for years in a cottage just north of Kielder Village with her Labrador dog, her goats and her ducks.

Janet told me how one Sunday in the Kielder church, just as the service was about to begin, my Aunt Belle arrived and announced in a loud voice "my ducks need a fellow!" There was a sudden silence, and a look of shock on all the faces of the well-dressed elderly congregation!

This year I was not going through the outskirts of Edinburgh then having to get a lift over the Forth Bridge as I did in 1989. I had arranged to go and see Betty Reed and her son Robert who used to farm near me. They had sold their farm and taken over a hotel near Biggar, so instead of going north from Peebles, we went on west to Biggar to visit them.

From Biggar it was north to Carnwath, through Shotts, past its prison and remand centre then east of Airdrie and up towards Cumbernauld. There were some grim areas to go through with fly tipped rubbish dumped along roadsides and some aggressive drivers on the roads, but

there were some helpful, kind, friendly people along the way so I had no problem finding somewhere to camp.
We got to Stirling and guided by more helpful people, got through all the under-passes under the main roads, then over the old bridge to Bridge of Allan. My plan was to head towards Callander to join a cycle route I had been told about that went north to Killin.

There was no avoiding a lot of travelling on roads to get to Callander which seemed to be full of tourists, but I did eventually find someone who could direct me to where they said I could join the cycle route just before the Pass of Leny. What a relief, I thought it will be to get off busy roads.
Sure enough, there was the entrance to the cycleway, but oh dear, there was a locked gate right across the entrance with only a narrow opening at one side to squeeze a bike through. There was no hope of getting a horse through it even if I took all the packs off.
A cyclist arrived and pushed his bike through the narrow opening, then saw me with Jester and said "if you go on up the road, there is another entrance with no locked gate across it." I looked at my map and saw where the entrance was, but it was going to mean going up the main road through the Pass of Leny.
Back we went to the main road. It was awfully busy with lots of coaches, speeding cars and heavy vehicles. As we got towards the Pass, the road got narrower with rocks at the side. Vehicles squeezed past us and didn't seem to slow down at all, and no way were the drivers going to wait as an oncoming vehicle headed towards us. They drove on between us and the oncoming vehicle. As a huge bus overtook us just when another bus was coming the other way, I really thought we were going to be crushed against the rocks!
Having survived that, and breathing a sigh of relief, I suddenly saw a van overtake another bus heading towards us. I don't think the driver of the van had seen us and was taking advantage of a pause in the traffic coming up behind us. He headed straight at us, then swerved just avoiding us and not hitting the bus he was overtaking!! "Never again," I said to Jester

as we turned into the entrance to join the cycle route. Jester and I were both in a sweat from the frightening ordeal, but we soon calmed down as we went on up the track alongside Loch Lubnaig. It all looked so calm and beautiful.

Away across the Loch I could see traffic racing along on the main road and felt thankful we were no longer having to face it. The cycle route took us past Strathyre Village and on to Balquhidder.

I found a nice grass area to camp and was just about to unload Jester when a voice called out "You can't camp here! We don't allow camping!" I explained that I only wanted to stop for the night and thought as it was an unfenced area off the road, no-one would mind. After chatting for a while I was told it would be alright just for the night. Then as I got the tent up and everything inside it, I was brought some eggs for my supper!

I had been warned that after Balquhidder there were locked gates across the cycle track with narrow side openings with cattle grids across them, so I wouldn't be able to get a horse through, but if I contacted a local farmer he would let me across his land.

We got into Balquhidder the next morning and I found a telephone box and rang the farmer. Yes, that would be alright, but I would need to go up a forest track to a gateway out of the forest onto his land. We followed the Forestry Commission track to where the farmer told me there was the gate onto his land. We came to a new fence that looked as if it had very recently been constructed. I could see a new stile over the fence but no sign of a gate. The forest track ended and all I could see was a new wire fence, no sign of a gate, only the stile ahead of us. There was nothing we could do but turn back and go to Balquhidder.

I looked at my map. If we went further on along the road from Balquhidder and tried the cycle track, again it would be impossible to get a horse along it because of the locked gates and cattle grids across the narrow opening at the sides. The only other alternative was to go on to the main road and along it to where it looked possible to join the cycle route again after crossing the farmer's fields.

We continued on along the road from Balquhidder towards the main road. As we got nearer and could hear the roar of traffic, I could feel Jester getting tense, and I am sure he could feel the tension in me. The sun came out. It was beautiful! I had to keep telling myself "be grateful it isn't raining and you don't have traffic spraying wet over you as they speed past!" What a relief getting back onto the cycle route before it went down the hill into Killin.

We hadn't gone far when we met a young lady pushing her bike up the steep slope. She was only using one arm as her right arm was in a sling. She stopped to talk to me. When I told her how dangerous I found the traffic on the roads, she explained why her arm was in a sling. "A car hit it when speeding past me on my bike far too close to me, and broke it." She then went on to tell me how lucky she had been that only her arm was broken! She knew of three people who had been killed after being hit by a vehicle while cycling along the road.

We were making our way to join our 1989 route through Glen Tromie from Dalnacardoch to Kingussie. I rang the keeper at Dalnacardoch and he organised getting the two locked gates across the track unlocked for me. I made sure the saddlebags were evenly balanced this time so they did not tip sideways, then with care, we managed to cross the river before Gaick without the bank giving way.

After having to turn back because of the locked gate north of Aviemore in 1989, then ending up having to go through Aviemore, I decided to go along back roads to Carbridge. After Carbridge I could join the cycle route through Slochd on the old A9.

We camped on the way on a grassy area by a derelict farm. I had the tent pitched by an old barn and Jester tethered to an old fence post nearby. All was peaceful. We were out of the wind and it wasn't raining. Owls were hooting in the trees nearby as I was lulled off to sleep. Then suddenly I woke up to the sound of hooves followed by squealing horses. I grabbed my glasses which immediately steamed up as they were so cold when I put them on, then fumbled about to find my torch and staggered out of the tent. I could see two horses charging round Jester as he pranced about at the end of his tethering rope.

What was I going to do? If those horses got their legs wound up in Jester's tethering rope, the situation could end up a disaster with lame horses. I certainly didn't want Jester injured!

With a lot of shouting and swearing at the horses to keep them away from Jester, I managed to get hold of him and drag him into the barn, then heaved the rickety old door closed as far as I could so no horse could get through. There was nothing I could do about the two loose horses, but hoped they would not trample on my tent. Fortunately they were only interested in trying to get to Jester in the barn.

As soon as it was daylight, I could see an open gate into a field nearby. With a lot more shouting and swearing I managed to get the two horses into the field and close the gate.

Rain was pouring down so I tied Jester up in the barn, then ran to and fro until I got everything out of the tent and onto Jester's back. I carried Piglet into the barn, then took down a very wet tent and strapped it behind the saddle on Jester's back. I put a reluctant Piglet into her saddlebag, covered Jester with the waterproof sheet and off we went.

I had arranged to go and visit Deborah whose wedding I had been to in 1990 (when Jester, after we set off on a trip to Ireland, had got into the feed shed, eaten all the hen corn, then ended up lame). Deborah now lived on the Black Isle north of Inverness. To get to the Black Isle I had a choice: to go through Inverness, then join Scotland's main road north which went over the Beauly Firth on the Kessock Bridge, or go away round the Beauly Firth through Kirkhill and Beauly. Going away round the Beauly Firth was going to take a lot longer. Looking at my map it looked possible to get through Inverness on back roads, but to go over the Kessock Bridge with all the main road traffic would be scary for both Jester and myself. I decided we would go the long way round through Beauly. It did seem a long way and a long slog on a main road, but once through Beauly and onto a quiet road along the north shore of the Beauly Firth, with the sun shining, it was beautiful. Inverness looked spectacular over the water and the Kessock Bridge looked magnificent in the distance. The vehicles on the huge iron structure looked like mini models crossing over it.

We got to Deborah's that night and I put up my tent in the garden and tethered Jester on a grass area by some trees nearby. Deborah already had a house full of visitors, but I joined them all for supper – after having a welcome bath.

After a few nights camping in Deborah's garden, we continued on north through Dingwall, then the back road to Evanton and on towards Bonar Bridge as the rain began to pour down.

Drivers were driving past us at speed on the wet road. The fast-spinning wheels made a loud whooshing noise as they hit the water and sprayed us, which was very frightening for Jester. As the rain continued to pour down, more water collected on the road making the situation even worse. We got to Bonar Bridge where the traffic was slower, so Jester calmed down a bit, but after Bonar Bridge drivers seemed to drive even faster! The on-coming traffic was the worst. The sound, then the sight of spraying water made Jester try and spin around and bolt away from them. How glad I was we could get off the main road at Invershin and go along a back road to Lairg.

It was getting late in the evening as we headed north from Lairg. We turned onto the road that went along the north side of Loch Shin and there was a farm on our right with a lovely overgrown grass area between the farm buildings and the road. I turned Jester in and we went up to the farmhouse beyond the building and I knocked on the door. A man opened the door and I pointed to the grass area and said "would you mind if I camped there for the night?"

"Yes, I would mind" came an abrupt reply. So I said I had better go on up the road and find somewhere else.

"That's all my land as well," came another abrupt reply.

I tried explaining what I was doing and only wanted to stop for the night then go on north next morning, but got an even sterner look and no reply!

Then I said "it is going to get dark soon, I had better go on and find somewhere to stop."

Suddenly he said "Just for the night?"

I confirmed "Just for the night" and then he said, "Well, just for the night, but you better be off first thing in the morning."

I agreed and hoped it was not going to still be pouring with rain in the morning.

It was not raining, all was quiet as I woke, then began getting my things sorted out inside the tent and into the saddlebags, when Mr. "Grumpy" appeared striding past with a mass of dogs and called out:

"You're nearly off then?"

"Yes," I replied as I tried to crawl out of the tent to thank him but he briskly strode on. Either he didn't hear me or didn't want to. He certainly wasn't going to stop!

We were heading towards Durness. The single-track roads were a relief as there really was not enough room for a vehicle to pass Jester with the saddlebags on him. Either drivers pulled into a passing place when they saw us, to let us pass, or waited until I turned Jester into a parking place to let them pass us. There was always a friendly wave of thanks and often as we got alongside each other, a driver would wind down the vehicle window and have a chat.

To find a camping place with enough good grass for Jester to eat was difficult. We had a night by Loch More sharing the grass area with many red deer. All was calm – such a picturesque spot with the moon shining on the loch, rutting stags roaring and the rippling sound of the water against the edge of the loch.

I had not been asleep long when I awoke to the sound of the water, like waves, crashing against the banks at the side of the loch. The wind had got up and as it got stronger, the sound of the water got louder. I could no longer hear the roar of the rutting stags. Camping in a high wind in an open area can be a bit frightening. There is always the danger of it getting worse and of me ending up lying awake wondering if the tent is going to survive!

As a complete contrast the following night the only good grass area I could find before dusk was next to Rhiconich sewage pump. It was beautifully sheltered and Jester appreciated the good grass!
After that it was a very wet plod in persistent rain to Durness.
I was glad to find a well stocked shop where I could get much needed provisions when we got there. It was early afternoon but the three of us had had enough so I asked the lady serving me in the shop if she could suggest a place to camp when a man's voice from behind me said "You are welcome to camp on my farm down at Balnakeil."
As we followed his directions to his field, the rain stopped and out came the sun. When Jester saw the lush grass, he could not wait for me to get all the packs off him.
By the time I got the tent up the sun was getting really so bright it was drying all my damp things.
Piglet and I lay in the sun until Jester had filled himself up with enough grass then I managed to get myself stimulated enough to get out the spare set of hind shoes from the saddlebags and replace the worn-out ones on Jester's hind feet which were so thin they would not have lasted another day's wear on the roads.
Jester was ready to graze again after that and I joined Piglet lying in the sun.
Suddenly we were jolted from our oasis of peace into the reality of today's world by the deafening blast of high-powered jet engines; then two low flying aircraft roaring over us like angry alien monsters.
Jester was terrified and bolted off down the field. Piglet sat shaking with fear and the air became heavy with a haze of polluting fumes.
How ironic I thought, realizing these two low flying, polluting angry monsters, that shattered our peace, were most probably on a Ministry of Defence peace-keeping training exercise.

The next day we followed the road round the coast to Eriboll in brilliant sunshine. We stopped to picnic just past the Eriboll Estate Farm where I sat looking across the water towards the far shore we had just come down. All looked so stunningly beautiful I didn't want to move on again, but it was now October, daylight hours were getting shorter and we had an awful long way to go before we would get home. We turned south down the road alongside Loch Hope then I started looking for a place to camp for the night.

I could see cattle grazing away ahead of us. Normally, I won't camp where there are cattle as they can be so inquisitive and end up trampling on the tent.

As we got nearer to them, they suddenly saw us approaching then spun round and fled off into the distance and away out of sight. I don't think they had ever seen a pack horse before and doubted they would come back again, so as it was getting late I decided to stop and pitch the tent.

The grass was not so good for Jester so I gave him the rest of the carrots I had got from the Durness shop. Piglet and I then got ourselves comfortable in the tent and it wasn't long before we were both asleep.

There isn't a lot of room in my light-weight "one man" tent with two large saddlebags and Piglet alongside me.

During the night I awoke as I was trying to turn over in my sleeping bag without squashing Piglet. What was that I heard? Plop, plop, plop! Then I heard it again; plop, plop, plop. And there it was again, plop, plop, plop. It sounded awfully like cows doing cow pats very near my tent. Had they come back again after all?

I tried to persuade Piglet to go out and chase them, but no, she was not going out of the tent. She refused to move at all so I decided I had better go out myself and chase them away before they got nearer the tent.

After groping about to find my glasses and then my torch and struggling to get my boots onto my feet, I crawled out of the tent. The moon was shining on the water, but there was no sign of any cattle anywhere – but there was that plop, plop, plopping sound again. It was coming from the edge of the water of the loch.

I walked over towards where the sound was coming from and there were two rowing boats moored on the water's edge and a slight breeze was blowing the water against them. As they rocked with the movement of the water it was going plop, plop, plop against their sides. It really did sound very like cows doing pats, but fortunately it was not but once back in my sleeping bag I drifted off to sleep dreaming of cows getting near the tent and hearing them doing pats beside it then about to walk onto the tent.

We were making our way back to Lairg after a night camping at the Crask Inn, lulled to sleep by the chug, chug, chug of its generator and the sound of rutting stags roaring in the background.

Next morning we continued on down the road and were not far from where we turned west up the road alongside Loch Shin on our way north, I saw a tractor coming towards us. The driver looked familiar – and it was Mr Grumpy! He did manage a wave as he passed us. Not long afterwards I heard a tractor coming up behind us at an alarming speed. Surely, I thought it will slow down as it passes us, but it didn't. It was Mr Grumpy again. He didn't manage a wave this time. I wondered why he was going so fast. Was he trying to get back to his farm before us in case I wanted to camp there again?

We got back to Lairg and I tied Jester up outside the grocer's shop and went in to stock up again with carrots, porridge oats, cheese oatcakes and milk.

I had just got through the door when a lady came up to me. "I'm Joyce, will you please come and have coffee with me at the Gallery just round the corner? You can put your pony in the garden and you must bring your dog in with you."

Once I had got my shopping into the saddlebags, I led Jester round the corner and found the Gallery.

"Come on in," a voice called. So I let Jester graze on an overgrown lawn, took Piglet out of her saddlebag and followed Joyce inside and was handed a mug of coffee.

"I must just pop round and tell Auntie to come and meet you," she said and was off through the door calling out "whatever you do don't mention anything about age to Auntie."

I put my mug of coffee on the table and Piglet and I waited. Suddenly the door flew open and in came an elderly lady with bright red hair, clutching a Chihuahua under her arm and holding a bag of carrots. She put the Chihuahua on the table and it immediately pushed its nose into my coffee. As Auntie marched out of the door declaring she must feed Jester the carrots, the Chihuahua suddenly squatted down and urinated on the table right beside my mug of coffee.

I abandoned the coffee and followed Auntie into the garden to find her pursued by Jester who was demanding more carrots.
"No, no, that's enough …. No that's enough" she kept telling him as she retreated backwards trying to get away from him. Poor Auntie, she looked terrified then very relieved when I got hold of him so she could escape back to the Gallery.
We left Lairg and continued on down the back road past the Shin Falls then it was back to wider roads – no more single track roads with passing places; no more friendly waves or stopping for a chat. It was as if drivers' attitudes changed completely once they were driving on wider roads. There seemed to be a sudden urgency to speed up and get to wherever they were going as quickly as possible.
Jester thought the sudden change was frightening. I could feel him getting more and more tense whenever speeding vehicles came past us, many of them alarmingly close to us.
When we got to the Black Isle to camp for a night in Deborah's garden, she handed me a photocopy of two off-road routes a friend of hers had given her as suitable for me to ride along on the way home. One route

looked really interesting going south from Fort Augustus over the Corrieyairack pass. The other off-road route was along the north side of Loch Ness but not all the way to Fort Augustus. I would have to go onto the A82 some of the way – "a very dangerous road" a cyclist had warned me, then explained how a cycling friend of hers had got killed by a large wagon getting too close to her bicycle then crushing her to death. The alternative was to go along the less busy roads on the south side of Loch Ness but to get to the south side I would need to go away round by Beauly again or ride over the Kessock Bridge.

I rang Inverness police. "Yes," I was told, "you can, provided you keep to the cycle lane."

"Right Jester, we are going over the Kessock Bridge."

The roar of A9 traffic had Jester wide awake. We followed a good cycle lane up to the bridge, Jester walking faster and faster. Piglet was getting shaken up and down in her saddlebag.

Once on to the bridge, Jester was all for charging forward to get to the other side as quickly as possible but with a firm hold of the reins, I managed to keep him at a "jogging" walk. "Great" I thought, we are doing well, when suddenly I realised the strap holding Piglet's saddlebag in place had given way. I just managed to grab her before she fell. There was a very scary moment when I was struggling to hold onto Piglet with one hand and control Jester with the other hand. If he had shot forward out of control with all that traffic alongside us, the packs could have all come off and probably Piglet and myself as well.

Jester was dripping with sweat as we got to the other side. I managed to turn onto a back road and stop and fasten Piglet's saddlebag in place with a spare boot lace, then somehow we found our way along side streets and roads onto the south side of Loch Ness.

After a night camping near Foyers we continued on towards Fort Augustus then turned up a side road just south of the town and came to a notice pointing up a stone track with "Old Military Road" written on it.

I learnt later it was a military road built by British soldiers under General Wade as part of a link road system to allow swift deployment in times of trouble during the Jacobite uprising, in an attempt to restore the Stuart dynasty to the British throne.

At last we were away from roads and traffic. I could let Piglet out of her saddlebag. She went bouncing off ahead full of excitement, then came rushing back to see where Jester and I had got to.
Jester decided as the track got steeper that it was too steep for him to carry me plus all the packs. He stopped and waited for me to get off him and lighten the load. As I dismounted I glanced back down the hillside and there way below was Fort Augustus and Loch Ness. What a fantastic view! It did look beautiful.
When we got higher up a damp mist kept creeping over us. Then as the track levelled out before we started going down the other side, huge ugly pylons loomed out of the mist like massive giants peering at us.
It was very slow going down the other side. The track had been badly damaged by years of severe winter weather. Rocks and huge boulders were across it and in one area the track was so eroded it was difficult to find. It took us five and a half hours to get to the single track tarmac road that led down to Laggan village.
It was now October 20th. I had decided to go back by Tomintoul and through Ballater which meant heading north again for a few miles from Newtonmore and Aviemore before we could go south to Tomintoul.
We stopped to camp one evening not far from Aviemore and I put the tent up in pouring rain. It was bitterly cold and the rain turned to sleet, then snow.
Next morning I was pleased to see there was only a thin covering of frozen snow on the ground and there was no mention of more snow when I listened to the weather forecast on my pocket radio.

I got Jester tacked up and the saddlebags onto him, but the tent was so frozen it would not wrap up. I shook it and a layer of ice fell off it like broken sheets of glass, then I slung it over the back of the saddle.
I picked up a shivering Piglet and put her in her saddlebag as we had to go on roads yet again, so she was safely out of the way of traffic.

Just as Jester stepped forward I happened to glance down at his front feet. Oh horrors! "Jester, you've lost a shoe." He had been grazing loose on a large rough area. There seemed no point in searching for it and he couldn't go miles along roads with no shoe on one front foot. I would have to get out the emergency shoeing tools and a spare fore-shoe from the saddlebags and put it on his foot.

With frozen hands in the bitter cold it was a real struggle to get it nailed on. I had to keep reminding myself that at least I could do it. If I had had to find a blacksmith and arrange for him to come and do it, we could have been stuck in the cold draughty spot for another night.

We got to Tomintoul that night and camped in the village field. The sun came out briefly during the day and melted the snow, but it was another bitter cold night.

Once in the tent, Piglet and I were snug and warm, but we both found it hard to get motivated into action in the morning when it was so cold.

We left Tomintoul in the morning but again we had to keep to the road as Glen Avon Estate were not going to let me go down the Glen with a dog.

It was a long steep climb up over the Lecht. As we got higher and higher, the snow got deeper and deeper. Then a snow plough passed us pushing piles of snow into the roadside. As it went ahead out of sight several cars passed us – then another, and another, and another followed by several more.

It wasn't until we got to the top and saw people skiing down a ski slope and cable cars full of people being taken back up again, that I realised why the road was so busy.

As Jester and I were watching all the skiers neither of us realised there was a cattle grid across the road directly ahead of us.

We came to a sudden stop, then I looked for a side gate. All I could see was snow piled up on each side. If there was a side gate, it had to be under all the snow. Even if I did find it, I would never be able to open it.

I turned round then saw a short way back we could get into where there was a variety of wooden buildings below the ski slope. We got in alright, but to find a way to the other side of them where I could see a car park, we had to climb up towards the ski lift with its cages full of skiers whizzing up and down above us.

Jester was terrified. We shot past and into the car park when a voice called out "That's a Haflinger." Then a man came striding towards us.

"I'm from Austria and I breed Haflingers," he called, then stood and looked at Jester.

"Now that's what they are meant for," he said, looking at all the packs on Jester, then laughing at Piglet in her saddlebag.

I had hoped to go up Glen Muick from Ballater then over the top to Glen Clover but "No, not today as we are shooting up there," I was told.

Instead we went round by Fettercairn and Edzell, Kirriemuir, Caputh, then Bankfoot near Perth to see some friends I knew there. After that it was down to Auchterarder crossing the A9 at Blackford. Fortunately that part of the A9 was not yet dual carriageway but it was still a dangerous crossing. Vehicles went so fast it was difficult to gauge when there was time to cross.

We got there and waited until the road seemed clear, then when I was just beginning to tell Jester to go quickly forwards, vehicles would suddenly appear racing towards us, and I would have to pull him back. We made several attempts to cross over then managed to make a dash for the other side only just getting across as vehicles raced past behind us.

Over Sherriff Muir and we were back onto the route we came on going north, under all the underpasses in Stirling then heading towards Cumbernauld.

How lovely it was to be in brilliant sunshine as we came over towards Kilsyth from Carron Bridge. Then we came to Abronhill, a housing estate on the outskirts of Cumbernauld and made our way to the little road that goes by Fannyside Lochs. The sun was still shining, but what it was shining on made me groan with disgust. All the piles of fly-tipped rubbish dumped along the roadside in the nearby woods, in the ditches, in gateways and spilling out onto the road. It made the whole atmosphere of the area depressing; as if the sun that had brightened and cheered up the day had been blotted out.

Litter strewn along all the roadside verges then we would pass another heap of fly-tipped rubbish. We needed somewhere to stop so Jester could graze and Piglet and I have our lunch, but there was nowhere free from litter or disgusting dumped rubbish.

We were coming into Shotts. As well as all the litter everywhere, the traffic was awful! I was getting angry and thinking "what a lot of thoughtless people there are in this area," when there, just back off the road, was a lovely open space with plenty of litter-free grass. I got off Jester and lifted Piglet down out of her saddlebag when I noticed a man walking across to watch us from what looked like a large garage beyond the grassy area.

My immediate thought was "he's going to object to me stopping here," so I called out "is it alright to stop and graze my pony for a while?" "Yes of course it is, and you are welcome to stay as long as you like," he called back to me. Then he came and looked at Jester with all the packs on his back and asked all about what I was doing.

As we chatted, a lady arrived with some extra feed for Jester. As she chatted a man arrived to ask if he could bring me some hot soup his wife had just been making. The thoughtful friendly atmosphere they brought was like a curtain being lifted to let the sunshine back in again.

There was not much sunshine during the rest of our journey home. It was November 6th by the time we got back. Daylight hours got so short, progress was slow and made even slower on wet miserable days when the mornings and evening were so dark.

We were all three of us glad to get home. Then it was back into the riding school routine which Jester and I always found difficult at first, but it soon became back to normal as if we had never been away!

8

Journey to Southern Ireland 1993

Over the fifty years of these journeys with a pack pony, I have always taken a notebook with me on each trip and written in it daily a diary of my travels.
These notebook diaries have been pushed into a drawer after each trip and not opened again until several friends suggested I wrote a book about my travels.

It has taken me a number of years to get enthusiastic enough to get started. Was anybody going to be interested enough to read a book about someone they didn't know who went away each year on a camping trip to different parts of the country with a pack pony? I wasn't convinced that they would, but when I did eventually rummage through the stack of notebooks filling the drawer below my desk and began reading through some of them, I was surprised how much it jogged the memory and brought back so much I had forgotten about.

Now writing this third book, I have just got out the notebook headed "1993 Journey to Southern Ireland" and opening it find I had completely forgotten I had written about the whole trip in rhyme.
At first I thought "I cannot put it in verse in the book I am writing." That was going to mean changing it all to prose. Now having read it through, I have decided to write it out just as it was written then! So here it is:

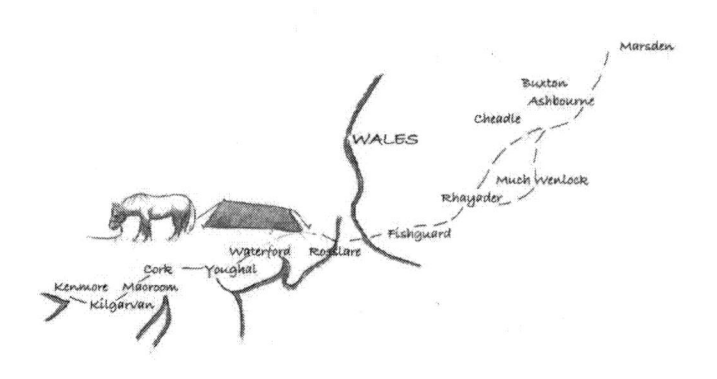

JOURNEY TO KENMORE 1993

written as I walked along leading Jester!

I'm going to try to write in rhyme
as going my journey this time
Feel I want to give it a try
because you see I'll tell you why
it's the clip clop of Jester's feet
that gets me in the rhythmic beat.

Monday morning 6th September
was there more I should remember?
The saddlebags could hold no more,
I took them out and closed the door.
Loading all onto Jester's back
trying hard to balance each pack
or else it would begin to slip
and over Jester's side would tip.
When that happens it is a pain
all must come off and start again.

Heading south we were on our way,
a dark and uninspiring day.
The Blanchland moors' scent of heather
compensated for the weather.

Before Middleton in Teesdale
our energy began to fail
so headed for a grassy space
for Jester and tent ideal place.
Piglet had run with us all day
chasing rabbits along the way.

A tired dog flopped in the tent
but phew what a disgusting scent!
In what dead matter had she rolled,
not to roll she will not be told.
The sort of smell we hate to greet
to a dog is a special treat!

Cleaned down with antiseptic wipe
made the smell a less odorous type.
To sounds of Jester grazing grass
the last daylight began to pass.

I slipped into my sleeping bag
and soon my eyelids began to sag.

From Teesdale to North Yorkshire moors
a fav'rite area of my tours
but alas so much heavy rain
from darkened sky with force it came,
and however hard I did try
t'was impossible to keep dry.
New Gore-Tex boots soaked in the rain,

and down my neck wet did the same.
Wet socks rubbed and made my feet sore
and more wet days made my blisters raw.

Onto the bleak Oxenhope moor
where mist kept opening like a door
showing huge windmills all around
ploughing the air without a sound.
Some new wind generating scheme
like weird ghosts they did seem.
A dry place tonight for my bed
along the back of a cow shed.
At Uncle Taylor's farm we were,
camped here now for some twenty year.
The evening spent by Taylor's fire
his tales of past I never tire.

Over the hill into Marsden
where the town fair had just begun
Now safely up on Jester's back
fitted into the saddle-pack
Piglet spent part of the day
to keep her out of traffic's way.

The road took us right through the fair
sight of Piglet made people stare.
Jester alarmed at all the fun
loud music and huge things spun.

Towards Saddleworth moor now we climb
just as the sun began to shine.
Then great black clouds kept sweeping past
and upon us their showers cast.
Over the Pennines we did climb

up toward the bridleway sign.
Along lanes and tracks we went
over-looking Stalybridge we spent
the night camping at Sun Green Farm.

Morning greeted us dry and calm
but not very long did it last
as into Derbyshire we had passed,
Through the Goyt Valley in the rain
then we had to climb up again.
Rain and wind beat us with such force
I clung onto a frightened horse.
The rain and wind beat on us so
we could hardly see where to go.

On wind-swept and bleak boggy moor,
it's frightening when you are not sure.
I did know the way well enough
but the going was very rough.

It made the packs begin to slide
the wind's force blew them to one side.
Every few steps I had to stop
before the packs began to drop
to push them back in their place
so we went even slower pace.

Daylight then beginning to go
which made going even more slow.
In darkness to my sister's farm.
She had begun to feel alarm
as it grew dark and there no sign
"where's that stupid sister of mine?"
A welcome bath and lots of food

but Jester in the wet he stood
as no room in the stable there
so wind and rain he had to bear
but with a feed of lots of oats
and in one of my home-made coats.
Next day with weather still severe
"Jane you better stay on here."

After days of soaking sore feet
I went to buy myself a treat.
A lift to Buxton where I found
new boots for nearly sixty pound.
A lot of money yet for sure
but my feet from wet were secure.

Still it rained and wind did blow
by next day I felt we must go
or we would not get all the way
to our south west Ireland stay.

In chilly wind and lasting rain
the three of us set off again.
Slowly the weather did improve
and waterproofs I could remove.

Of pigs Jester has a real fear
even the smell he hates to be near
but when in front one does appear
he used to spin round with a rear.

Now he stands and stares with alarm
in great fear they will do him harm.
For some reason I'm not sure why
pigs kept as pets and not in sty

often wander freely about
pot bellied sort with crumpled snout.

Quietly one day one did appear
running along at Jester's rear.
First he did not catch sight of it
when he did poor chap had a fit.
He thought the pig was in full chase
and fast from it he had to race.
It really did damage his nerve.
After that made many a swerve
imagined pigs behind him came,
he kept seeing it back again.
Just as his nerves were nearly healed
there ahead of us in a field
two pigs arrived wanting their feed.
Strength to hold Jester I did need,
and so his nerves were frayed once more
and ghosts of pigs again he saw,
and so often it surprised me
a pig instead of a sheep he'll see.
Fortunately in Wales we've seen
that pigs are few and far between
and now we all do see the same

all sheep have become sheep again.
In this world of so much distress
mostly we hear about its mess.
The news that people want to tell
the media they do it so well
is of the horrifying sort
in negative trap we get caught.

Of people it makes one despair
I wondered if it's really fair
so many people I do find
of a far more positive mind.
So much depends on how we give
in attitude to life we live.
It seems the base of all does fall
on thoughts of why this life at all.

Round south of Cheadle now we come
winding on many a country lane
then to busier roads again
just as there came some heavy rain.

In the wet my map I misread
which took us too far south instead
that meant we had to double back
to find another north west track
which did arouse temper of mine
as wasted energy and time.

As still it would persist and rain
it I could for my temper blame
but later when the sun came out
the fuss I soon forgot about.
Leaving the Kerry hills behind

a sheltered picnic spot to find.
The wind too cold for us to stop
on the misty Kerry hill top.

We'd walked six hours without a break
about as much as we could take.
Our stomachs rumbled all around
tho' Piglet tasty yukkies found.
It's amazing what she will eat
and consider a tasty treat.
Her sense of taste like sense of smell
we in agreement don't do well.
After lunch on the way
we came to where I once did stay
camping on some rough grazing land
tethered Dexter bull near at hand.
Derelict cottage stood nearby
someone the roof had tried to tie
to hold old tin sheets in their place.
Broken glass hung from window case
the door was stopped with an old beam.
Through gaps yapping dogs could be seen.
Rubbish lay about everywhere
old cookers, beds, many a chair.

Imagine what was my surprise
when lady of rotunded size
told me the cottage was her home
where she and her dogs lived alone.

This time I found it no surprise
the rubbish had increased in size
but cottage and its whole entire
it had been finished by a fire.

She a rounder shape than before
I did meet there again once more,
living now in a caravan
building new house as best she can!
From what she said, as long I stood,
foundations were yet to be made good.
As two years since she had begun
hard to see when it would be done.

Towards Rhayader now we went
from peaceful night in forest spent.
In the busy Welsh market town
soon the saddlebags were weighed down
after I shopped for us more food,
as Jester by a pub he stood.

Then up onto the mountain road
very long steep climb we strode.
Beautiful country all around
echoing rushing water sound
cascading streams all full from rain
which on us it did fall again.

All the day there kept coming past
some were driving a bit too fast,
sheep in trailers, car, truck and van
fitted in however they can.
Builth Wells ram sales I was told
where some nine thousand rams are sold.
A very important sale indeed
all rams from every sort of breed.
For hundreds of miles farmers came
to sell rams and buy new again.
Wales to England so near at hand

yet people like from other land.
In foreign language they did confer
into English quickly transfer.
Children could do change about
in either language hear them shout.

All thoughts of pigs had nearly gone
o'er hundred miles since we saw one,
then pigs in a yard gave a squeal
as collie ran for Jester's heel.
All Jester saw was something big
and in his mind a collie pig
which gave him a tremendous shock
and me right over he did knock
then galloped off away ahead.
I'll not tell you now what I said.
Realising he was on his own
he went no further on alone.
Together again we then went
Jester sure pigs against him sent.

Near Temple Bar in pouring rain
then suddenly sun out again.
A car came and stopped in the road
from it a man and lady strode.
"We're from the Horse Protection League
your set-up does us so intrigue!"
As Jester then looked so depressed
he felt in want of food and rest.
I'm sure he would have agreed
had they said "that horse is in need!"
A magazine they then gave me
all of their work for me to see.
Looking at it along the way

shocking pictures it did display
suffering so bad I had to turn
around to Jester and confirm
although he had another thought
his suffering really came to naught!

Next night we camped on a farm
unsettled Jester showed alarm.
Unlike him he would stand and gaze
and not rush to the grass to graze.

It was later on I realised why
across the road pigs in a sty.
Then when the morning came
Jester was restless just the same.

When finding a pause in the rain
to pack up and be off again
was the time pigs were being fed
and many a squeal those pigs said.

With all the packs halfway on
then the pause in the rain had gone
so everything was getting wet
made me cross, Jester more upset.
So everything took twice as long
our time for off was well past gone.
That did not start the day so well
and to add to it more rain fell.
Then later on the rain did clear
and gave us all a feel of cheer.
Dried things out on a church yard gate
in sunny corner we all ate.
Cenarth Village was our next stop

to call at the post office shop.
A tourist spot as we soon saw
Piglet on Jester they adore
out come the cameras all around
lots of "oohs" and "aahs" and clicking sound.
Got away as fast as we could
but well stocked up with yet more food.

23rd September.
Our usual camp stop search
ended last night behind a church.
Lovely quiet peaceful place
an ideal grazing camping space.
A night without a drop of rain
but things do get wet just the same
because at this late time of year
cold nights and heavy dew appear.
In the tent the condensation
is as wet as if been rained on
but now today the sky has cleared
and brilliant sunshine has appeared
so all out drying in the sun
and our lunch we've just begun.
At Fishguard tonight we should be
then on to the Irish ferry.

We arrived in the haulier's yard,
just a few miles south of Fishguard.
Two weeks it's taken and three days
to ride down country all the way
from Northumberland into Wales
through lots of rain and awful gales.
Today the sun shone from blue sky
stopped to get all camping things dry

so all was wrapped dry and ready
to go tonight on the ferry.
At 3.00 am it would depart
that meant a very early start.

Jester was to load in the dark
before the ferry could embark.
In the trailer he had to stay
in the commercial vehicle bay.
Piglet lay curled up on the packs
which I had put in poly-sacks
in case t'was wet when we got there
unloading in rain at Rosslare.
There sure enough I was right,
The Irish rain was my first sight.

The trailer took us up the road
away from the docks to unload
onto a horse soaking with sweat
I loaded the packs in the wet.
The trailer left us to return
and we continued on our journ.

From the main road we cut across
over the hills towards New Ross
and then onto a quiet track.

From saddlebag on Jester's back
I lifted Piglet down to run
excited straight away she begun
to search for scent of a rabbit
as is every terrier's habit.
Through the town with just enough light
to a farm to camp for the night.

Main road again to Waterford,
over the bridge then head toward
quiet roads away from the race
of traffic that goes such a pace.

As near the outskirts of the town
onto a side road we went down
where rubbish lying all around
open grassy space we found
travellers of a different sort.
Children ran and around us fought
each one wanting to try and see
if they could beg money from me.
Then rid of them and on we strode
when a car came and blocked our road
and opening the window wide
a youth begged money from inside.
As I tried to lead Jester round
but in our way again he found.
"Not enough petrol to go far.
You give me money for my car."

Once more I did plainly refuse,
but wondered if he would abuse.
Instead he turned the car around
and went with a great revving sound.
With relief we continued on,
so very glad that he had gone.

But not a mile along before
there ahead of us I saw more
caravans parked beside the road
was where they had made their abode.
Over everywhere on the ground

all sorts of rubbish could be found
and people began to appear
when they saw we were getting near.
Lots of clothes on the hedge to dry
blew in the breeze made Jester shy.
He galloped ahead with alarm
scattered them all away from harm.
Not far past then he stopped to see
how far behind he had left me.
Heads peered out of caravan's door
but none ventured out as before
as I ran on ahead to get
a hold of Jester with Piglet.
To Dunhill where we did stop
and I went into the wee shop.
Then found Jester given some feed
which he ate as if much in need
and then they insisted on me
going in for a cup of tea.

A day with not a cloud to be seen
on all the sun shone supreme.
By Bon Machon on the shore
I could but only value more
with brilliance of the glistening sea
and all the picturesque country
how travelling along this way
when the weather is like today
brings out an appreciation
of the beauty of creation
on this planet we've been given
with a space of time to live in.
So much of life to me does seem
to rush like a cascading stream

that rushes on with such great force
it takes a fast more wearying course
than does the slowly rippling beck
that gently winds on peaceful trek.

Walking towards the setting sun
the coolness of the night begun
and as the daylight quickly fled
an amazing display of red
across the horizon ahead
gave a brilliant coloured spread.

We really needed now to find
before daylight left us behind
a suitable place for the night
but nowhere find a farm in sight.

We'd passed a man along the road
as quickly on ahead we strode.
With a sudden call from behind
made me quickly turn to find
the man we had just gone past
was running back towards us fast.
"You'd be needing somewhere to stay"
I heard him call towards our way.
"Follow me I have just the place
where you will have plenty of space
for your tent and tether your horse."

With the sound from the distant shores
of the sea now just out of sight
gratefully we settled for the night.
The plaintive sound that greets the dawn
an autumn tune somewhat forlorn

the robin sings beside my tent
telling me enough time is spent
and we must now start on our way
to get the most out of the day.

Piglet's stomach is quick to tell
it is her breakfast time as well.
Jester's call with nickering notes
telling me it's time for his oats.

And so another day began
in brilliant sun to Dungarvan.
Then cross country to Clashmore
many a horse on the road we saw
"You're now in racehorse country"
one of the riders said to me.
With them we briskly walked along
until the last of them were gone.
After that Jester went so slow
he said with them he'd rather go.
Youghal next by the sea again.

Superb view from the hills we came
but as we turned towards the town
all the traffic was slowing down.
Some major road works were ahead.
From steam rollers before we've fled.
Now three were there in front of us -
Jester too tired to make much fuss.
It was touch and go now and again
The worst was how the traffic came.
It made me think with some alarm
of girl I met with broken arm
knocked by a bus when on her bike

"About to be squashed it felt like."
Seems everyone's in such a rush
slowing for a horse is too much.
Hours of map reading I employed
some main roads we could not avoid.
Our route mostly along the way
on country roads and tracks we stay,
but country roads near a town
the traffic forgets to slow down.

Around Cork we now had to get
marked on my map a route I set.
On narrow roads on the north side
so from the town a distance wide.
Round here my map was out of date
less farms and more housing estate.
To their houses in their cars they came
along the narrow country lane
and littered along the hedgerow
is as if all their rubbish throw.
The same getting near any town
as if man's qualities run down.
There seems a general lack of care
of the land from which we do fare.

Over the hills north of Macroom
on a cold and wet afternoon
but clear enough on the hillside
to see the hills and country wide.
A most inspiring view ahead
upon our route we next will tread.
The morning came with heavy rain
beat on the tent without refrain.
Each time I peered out of the tent

sky showed no sign it would relent.
Above the rain about midday
I heard a voice call out and say
"Come across to the house please do
I have put some soup on for you too."
Now sitting by the kitchen fire
fascinated by the entire.
First thing on which my eye did fall
was a small red light on the wall.
Inside the light there was a cross
and above plaintive eyes looked across
from portrait of Christ hanging high
with picture of the Pope nearby.
Then around the table we all three,
the farmer and his wife and me,
compared notes on farming together
also the state of the weather.
With no break in the rain in sight
"You stay, camp here another night,
see if the weather does improve
in morning make an early move."
After heavy rain all through the night
all had gone quiet by daylight
only the wet squelching sound
of Jester's feet on sodden ground.

As grey clouds slowly cleared
amazing display of hills appeared
as we continued on our way
so grateful for a drier day.
Later a car was speeding past
like all Irish far too fast
Suddenly this tremendous bang
Jester took fright and off he ran.

Think it from car engine had come
sounded like a powerful gun.
Luckily the packs did not slide
and then slip over Jester's side
and away ahead he stopped to see
how far behind he had left me.

Over the hills to Kilgarvan
on back roads as much as we can
past fascinating little farms
with stacks of peat stored in barns.
Smoke from chimneys in the air
giving that scent elsewhere so rare.
Our journey's end we're nearly there
a few days we'll stay at Kenmare.
Then all the way back home we'll go
back before the winter snow.

With memories of this Irish land
which to me do first come to hand
either waterproofs on for the rain
or taking them back off again
and trying hard to stay alive,
because of the way the Irish drive
In prettiest land I have seen
with more friendly people never been.

---oo—

It was the end of October by the time we got all the way home from Southern Ireland. The grass had grown well in the main hay field since it had been cut for hay in July so I let Jester join the cows to graze it off before the frosty weather came and it lost its goodness.

One of the cows was due to calf during the first week of November, and she produced a lovely heifer calf. After a few days it was skipping round the field and bouncing up to Jester then would go racing back to its mother to get a feed of milk. Then as the days passed it spent more and more time with Jester only racing back to its mother when it decided it needed another feed of milk from her. Everywhere Jester went it followed him, then it would walk round him and get in his way so he would give it a nudge to push it to one side.

The friendship had to end as the winter weather progressed. The cows had to be moved to their winter quarters so they could have the cowshed to shelter in during bad weather.

By the end of February, the daylight hours get noticeably longer and the birds are beginning to tune up for their spring chorus. It is the time of year I begin to think of further journeys with a pack pony.

Jester, Piglet and I went on our usual visit to see Catherine at Drumstinchall at the end of May, so we could be back in time for the school Spring Holiday week.

Catherine was a great lover of birds and had an amazing variety of them feeding from all her bird feeders hanging outside the French windows of her living room. It was fascinating watching them all.

There was a badger living under her garage which came out in the late evenings and scuffled about under the bird feeders eating all the bits that had dropped on the ground.

Some evenings we would see a fox passing by on its regular route to wherever it went for its hunt for food.

We would often have interesting discussions together over all the wild life, nature and the countryside, but we differed in how we understood all these creatures as well as how all other forms of life came into being. Catherine believed all living things like her horses, all the birds on her feeders, that badger that dug out its sett under her garage, as well as the fox we often saw, had all evolved over millions of years from an earlier form of life, but I questioned, if that was so, how did all the different species come into being gradually from that original simple form of life? Did some decide to gradually develop over those millions of years into horses, some into birds and some into foxes or badgers? Years ago, I was given a book to read that I was told would help convince me Darwin was right with his belief of evolution. It was about a study that had been done of finches on the Galapagos Islands where it was noted that as the climate changed, birds that had larger beaks survived better than the others and this was meant to be evidence of life evolving. As far as I could see those birds were just adapting to the change in their environment. They were still finches.

It reminded me of a farmer I met up north who told me how he had bought some Devon cattle and wintered them out with his other cattle. During their first winter, they lost condition and didn't do at all well. By the next winter they had grown an extra thick coat of hair and did far better.

Were those cattle or those finches on the Galapagos Islands in the process of gradually, over many years, changing into something more developed? Surely they were just adapting to their changing environment.

I did hear that years later the finches on the Galapagos Islands with smaller beaks once again dominated the population.

No doubt if those Devon cattle were returned south again and away from the colder north their coats would become less hairy again in time.

We arrived home from Catherine's the day before the school holiday week. All my camping gear got put in a pile on the floor of my chalet, and there it stayed until the end of the busy week of children riding and trekking before it got sorted out ready for being used again in September.

By the middle of June I was listening to the weather forecast each day on my radio hoping to hear of a dry spell ahead so that I could make hay. The cows were in their summer field with access to the cow shed again. This time it was to shelter from the flies which pestered them relentlessly during the summer months. It was a good opportunity to get a halter onto the calf so that like my other cows, it learned to lead and be tied up. If I left it any longer, it was going to get too big and be able to pull or knock me over.

A calf's reactions to first being tied up is very different from the reactions of a foal. Calves do not try pulling backwards to get free, but instead they end up lying down and rolling their eyes and look as if they are dying!

I was a bit alarmed the first time I tied up a calf years ago. I expected it to react like a foal, but thinking about it, after tying up many future calves and foals, cattle's actions and reactions are overall not the same as horses. There are some similarities, but in the end all cattle have a basic way of behaviour common to cattle and horses have a basic way of behaviour common to horses in spite of each one's own individual character and really isn't that so with each species of animal or bird?

After the hay was made and safely in the hay shed and the busy school summer holidays were coming to an end, all the swallows that had nested in the stables and in the cow shed were lining up along the telegraph wires each day preparing for their annual autumn migration for the winter and then to return next spring. That instinctive pattern of life seems programmed into them.

Here I was preparing all I needed to go on a far shorter journey than those swallows were preparing for. They were taking no map or compass to make sure they were going in the right direction, no waterproof clothing, no porridge oats, no coffee, and none of the other essentials I was packing into the saddlebags to put on Jester to set off on our autumn journey in a few days' time. Watching those swallows made me think of my visits to Catherine and our evening discussions.

I cannot believe those swallows with their amazing instinctive pattern of life, can have developed through the process of evolution over millions of years from one original form of life. What directed them into the direction to go to develop from that original form of life to eventually become the swallows with their instinctive set pattern of life we see they have today, and what directed the original form of life to branch out in the direction to develop eventually into horses we see today and also to branch out in another direction to develop into cows – and also to branch out in yet another direction to develop into dogs, as well as branching out in differing directions to develop eventually over all those years into all the other varieties of other living species we see today?

9
Journey to Wales
1994

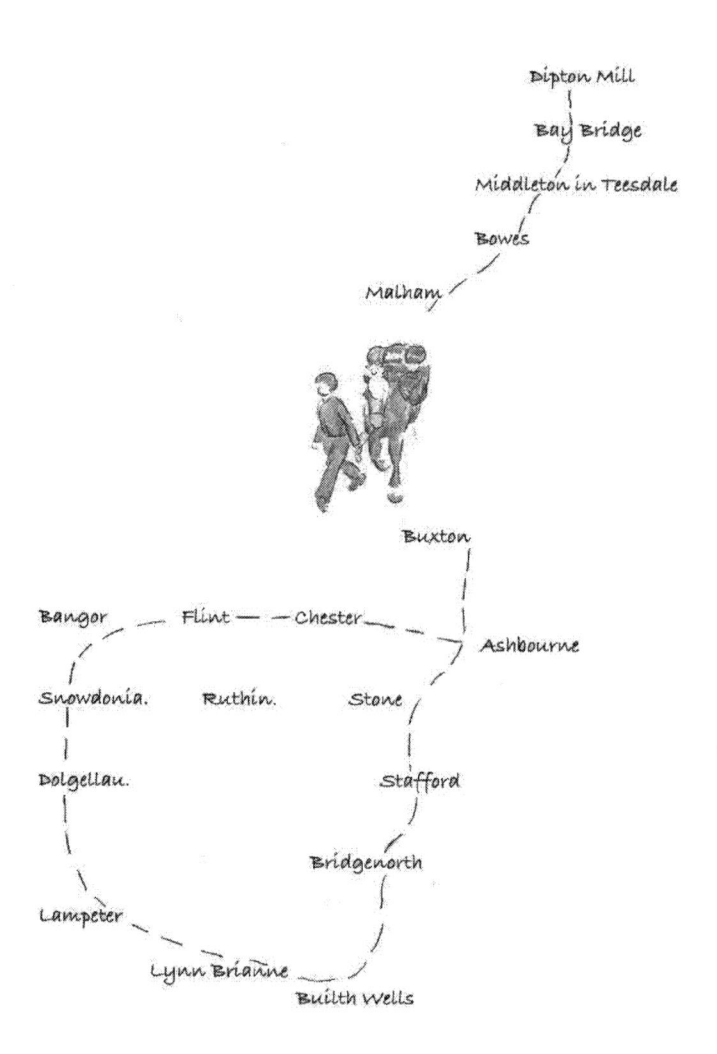

Dipton Mill
Bay Bridge
Middleton in Teesdale
Bowes
Malham

Buxton
Bangor — Flint — Chester
Ashbourne
Snowdonia. Ruthin. Stone
Dolgellau.
Stafford
Bridgenorth
Lampeter
Lynn Brianne
Builth Wells

It was Monday September 7th when Jester, Piglet and I set off on our 1994 autumn journey. We were heading south to go and stay with my sister in Derbyshire then to go on to explore more of the countryside of Wales.

There is always that feeling, for the first few miles of "I hope I've remembered everything" and "have I remembered to tell Chris where everything is that she'll need when she comes daily to see to the cows and the hens and to generally look after the place," or "should I have done this or that before leaving?"

Then as we get further on our way, there is that lovely feeling; "We are really on our way."

By the evening and we are at our first camping spot with the tent up and Piglet and I are inside with Jester grazing alongside on his long tethering rope, there is that thrilling feeling I get from looking forward to many days of camping and travelling.

After two lovely fine days, we were into the Yorkshire Dales. Next day the weather changed. We had just got started when down came the rain as the wind got stronger and stronger. I managed to find a sheltered camping place and the tent up then lifted everything off Jester as quickly as possible while the rain poured down. I got his waterproof sheet onto him then joined Piglet in the tent; took out my camping gas stove to brew up a hot drink; tried to light it, but it would not work.

I got out the spare gas cylinder to see if then it would work, but no, it still would not light. I fiddled about with it trying to see if I could find out what the problem was, but it was hopeless. I could not get it to light so gave up. I tried it again hopefully next morning, but no, it was not going to work.

It was no hot coffee, no hot porridge for two more cold, wet, windy days until we got to Marsden and I went into a shop that looked as if it might sell camping gas stoves.

"No, I'm sorry we don't stock them anymore. I think you would have to go into Huddersfield to get one."

Disappointed, I was walking out of the shop when a voice called out "wait a minute" and I turned round to see the shop assistant disappear out of sight. Soon she appeared back again carrying something. "Is this what you want?" and she handed me a camping gas stove.

"I suddenly remembered we had this one lying in the back for years from when we used to stock them, but nobody seemed to want them, so we stopped getting them."

Later as we plodded on in pouring rain, I noticed an empty shed so we went in and I got the new stove out of the saddlebags and brewed up a panful of hot coffee. What a wonderful mug of coffee that was!

That night in the tent as the rain still poured down, it was hot porridge for supper – delicious!

Next day was just as wet. Piglet was sitting in her saddlebag with her head peering out from under the waterproof sheet on Jester, when a lady came running out of a cottage holding a blanket and saying:

"That poor little dog looks so cold and wet." She wanted to wrap the blanket around Piglet as I tried to explain that Piglet was really snug and dry in her saddlebag. It was only her head that was wet.

I didn't want to end up with a wet blanket to carry.

We had a dry night in "Uncle" Taylor's cow byre. It is twenty years now since we first camped there. A frail old man of 92 years old now but still able to tell me tales of how he and his father, a cattle dealer, used to drive cattle on foot and hoof, all the way from Wales to Yorkshire.

He always insists I spend the evening with him in his cottage sitting by the fireside as he smokes his pipe, which he is continually lighting with an endless supply of matches. I think he ends up smoking more matches than tobacco. Then every so often there would be a hiss from the fire after he spat into it, then again get a match to relight his pipe before carrying on with yet more tales of the past.

Next day still it rained and we sloshed on over Saddleworth and eventually to Charlesworth where I was given a barn to camp in. Someone had stolen the old stone tiles off one end of the roof which was a shame as it was a lovely old barn. Piglet and I camped in the dry end and I was able to hang up some of my wet things to dry out a little overnight.

I had made a large waterproof for the trip to cover Jester with all the packs on him. Then it was to adapt to a waterproof sheet for him at night, but being large, it came right down over his tail so he could not lift it high enough when he pooed. As a result, all his poo got down his tail and with all the wet grass he was eating, it was wet sloshy poo down his beautiful flaxen tail!

Every so often I had to stop where there was some water so I could fill up my camping pan with the water and pour it down Jester's tail until it washed all the mess off it.

After studying my s to plan a route to the north of Wales from Buxton, I could see it was going to mean travelling along roads most of the way. I wanted to go across the north of Wales towards Bangor then go south to Llanberis and down the west side of Snowdonia.

Seeing a way along "quiet" roads on a map can be so different from when actually travelling on them. The traffic was so awful when we got there, I began to wish I had not decided to go to the north of Wales after all. Then later, feeling so grateful we had survived and not been mown down by reckless speeding drivers, we got to Flintshire where a farmer let me camp on a hillside overlooking the north coast with a fascinating view of Connah's Quay and Flint on a beautiful evening. I began to be glad I had decided to come into north Wales after all.

We had a night camping on a rough grassy area at the side of a lady's garden. She had two toddlers who were all excited and kept telling me "Daddy is coming home tonight!"

Later they brought Daddy down the garden to see me. They seemed so thrilled to show me their Daddy and were clinging to him as we chatted. I soon learned that Daddy no longer lived at home. He only came one evening a week to see the children.

I could see Mummy standing up by the cottage watching us as Daddy was explaining to the children it was now time for him to go and I wondered what those children's reaction must be when their super hero had gone and Mummy was left to cope on her own.

We were able to travel along bridleways over the hills as we headed west towards Llangernyw with some lovely views of the coast at Colwyn Bay and Conwy. The weather forecast for the night ahead was for gales and rain so I decided to make sure we could find a good sheltered place to camp.

We passed a farm near Mochdre, then I saw an open area near a stream beautifully sheltered by trees. I turned Jester around and went back to the farm and met a farmer coming out of one of the outbuildings and asked him if I might camp "over there" and pointed to the open unfenced area I had seen.

"Yes you can camp there, but what about your pony, as there is no fence?"

I explained how Jester tethered on a long rope and I would tie the rope to one of the trees.

It was only early afternoon, but all three of us were glad to have an early stop.
Later that afternoon, I took Piglet for a short walk and gathered mushrooms which I kept finding as we walked along a path through some fields.

Jester was very pleased to see us when we returned. I think he thought we were continuing on without him!
I put the bag of mushrooms down, then bent down to unzip the entrance to the tent and saw it was already unzipped half way. "How careless of me to leave it like that" I thought as I pulled the zip up its full length. Oh horrors! Chaos! The saddlebags had been raided. Everything was scattered about in the tent. Polythene bags that had food in were ripped open, and the contents eaten. It must have been that collie that was watching me put up the tent after we arrived. I grovelled about trying to clear up the mess. It was beginning to get dark, so I called Piglet to go into the tent with me, but she wouldn't go in. That seemed strange as she loved the tent and usually was straight in then curled up on the saddle blanket. I got myself inside, but oh what a smell! I got my torch out "Oh yuk!" I shouted out. There was dog wee all down the inside of the inner tent. I had left my sleeping bag spread out ready for the evening. The wee had just missed it, but there was a huge puddle right next to it. I mopped it all up as best I could in the torchlight.

Next morning the sun came out and I found an old bucket in a tatty shed, filled it with water from the stream then piled all my things outside the tent, took out the inner tent, and washed it then hung it out to dry.

It was still a bit damp by the time I had everything sorted out to go onto Jester, but it is often just as damp from condensation after cold nights. The collie had not touched my porridge oats or the coffee and I had a tin of evaporated milk, so Piglet and I had something to eat.

We continued on west over to Rowen and onto an old Roman road going over the hills. It was beautiful countryside with lovely views of the coast and across to the Snowdonia hills but I had to look through a mass of pylons and cables to see the view. They were dotted about all over, but I suppose that is how it has to be with our continual demand for electricity to operate all the "necessities" of life we need these days.

We were into October by the time we got to Llanberis. A pot-bellied farmer let me camp on his empty campsite. The camping season had really ended but he let me put my tent up and tether Jester. Then later that evening he arrived with a friend to see me as they were so interested in what I was doing.

The campsite bins had not been finally emptied. I had managed to prevent Piglet from creeping off to raid them, but while chatting to the farmer and his friend, she sneaked off and I had to go and find her. Old habits die hard!

Next day we were on a narrow singletrack road when a car came up behind us the driver blasting its horn at us over and over again. I thought "What an impatient sod that driver is," as I got Jester on into a gateway so we could let the car pass. It zoomed past us then stopped ahead in a layby and a lady got out and shouted at me "I've been looking for you for days, ever since someone reported seeing you miles away."

My immediate thought was "Oh dear, what I have done! Is she a policewoman in plain clothes?"

She pointed to Jester. "That's a Haflinger" she boomed at me.

"Yes" I thought. "I know that!" – was she going to accuse me of stealing him?

She proceeded to fire questions at me; where had I got him from, how was he bred, how old was he, did I own him?

Apart from the stupidity of blasting a horn behind a horse, I did not like the abrupt way she spoke to me as she threw questions at me, so I tried to walk on, but was told to wait until she had finished.

Eventually, she explained she was doing a survey on Haflingers in Wales and she ended up being quite helpful telling me of good offroad routes I could take which were not marked on my map.

We got to the bridleway up past the Youth Hostel at Llamberis – "The Telegraph Track" I was told it was called. There were lots of telegraph poles lying rotting at the side of the track.

We stopped to watch the train chugging up Snowdon but as it got higher up the hillside it disappeared into thick mist. Its passengers were not going to get a view from the top. When we got to the top of the track we were climbing up, there was a fantastic view away down the valley below.

I could see a small farm away ahead, so decided to go there and ask the farmer if he would let me camp for the night.

"Yes, I let people camp over there at the end of the track and charge 50p."

The end of the track opened out into a lovely level grass area, all surrounded by hills and a stream tumbled down alongside. It was superb and no-one to be seen, only sheep and birds and us.

Next morning I was sad to leave such a beautiful camping spot.

We had a very wet journey over the hills to Prenteg overlooking the coastline and Portmadoc where, during a short sunny spell, I could see the toll bridge with queues of traffic on it, which made me feel grateful to be on a bridleway with traffic far away from us.

We had a nasty busy road to go along near Maentwrog before getting onto another bridleway but this one obviously wasn't used. We had to scramble through overgrown grass, nettles and brambles, and I struggled to open unused gates tied up with wire and baler twine and a tangle of weeds and undergrowth trying to stop me opening them. When eventually I got the wire and string undone, we managed to get right through and came to a farm where the farmer let me camp.

Next day the rain poured down so we stayed put. Jester had his waterproof sheet on him. Piglet refused to venture out of the tent. How did she manage to last so long without having to go out for a pee? I eventually had to make her go out later in the afternoon.

Next morning I woke to find slugs everywhere – huge things – in my coffee mug, in the porridge pan, in my boots, in the saddlebags, crawling up inside the tent as well as outside it. I had to pull them off and out of my things. Then there was the ordeal of getting rid of their sticky slime that seemed impossible to get off my fingers.

We had more very wet days as we continued on South towards Dolgellau. We had a short distance on a main road one day, but it had no traffic racing along on it. Then ahead we came to two police cars and an ambulance. A policeman came to escort us past a wrecked car and said to me "we would all be better travelling your way."

I was having great difficulty reading my map in the pouring rain. My glasses were so wet I could hardly see through them, and the polythene bag I had the map in was all wet so I didn't chance the next bridleway, but kept on a quiet road until we came to a farm.

I found a shepherd training his dog and asked about somewhere to camp, but was told it was all estate land for the next few miles and the owner of the estate was away so I couldn't get permission to camp, but there was a campsite a few miles on down the road.

It was a long wet few miles before we came to a notice saying "Camping" and then another notice saying "Enter, pitch and the management will see you later." So we did enter and pitch and I tethered Jester to a tree. Piglet and I had just got into the tent when a voice called out "Hello." I poked my head out of the tent "You cannot camp here with a horse – you'll have to move on."

"But it's too dark to continue on" I replied.

"Well, you will have to make your horse's rope much, much shorter and I'll have to charge you for grazing as it's eating the grass for my sheep. That is £3 for the tent and £3 for the grazing."

I tried arguing as that was a lot more than I had ever paid anyone, but he gave me no choice.

"You pay it or you move on."

He even watched me shorten Jester's rope and kept saying "No, that is not short enough!"

Poor Jester could hardly move in the end but later when no-one was about, I lengthened it again.

Next morning still the rain poured down but we had to move as I had been told I had to leave first thing in the morning. He would have probably charged me more for grazing if he had seen Jester had eaten more of his sheep's grass.

Next day we went through Dolgellau and met crowds of people cheering as a runner passed us and I was told it was Ian Botham on some charity run!

We were towards Glashill, a beautiful area but so wet with rain pouring down. By late afternoon we had had enough so I called at a farm. Again it was an estate farm but the owner was a lady who lived in a huge mansion nearby. I led Jester up to the main door and rang the bell. A lovely lady came, opened the door and looked very surprised to see a wet horse with a dog's head peering out from under the waterproof sheet on it – then looking at me she said "You look so wet, do come inside."

I tied Jester up to the gate then was ushered into the kitchen and given Marmite sandwiches and a pot of tea. Then she said:

"I'll go and ring the manager and see where you can camp."

Soon after I was finishing my second cup of tea, the manager arrived and escorted me to a lovely sheltered place overlooking the valley below. The rain stopped and we got settled for a very comfortable night.

We left next morning and went down the "West Drive," sadly overgrown and hardly a drive any more, but still very beautiful.

We came to a gate which I tried to open, but it would only open so far then jammed as I was trying to push it and lead Jester through. I could hear the thump of the saddlebags hitting the gate, but the waterproof sheet must have caught on the gate. Jester shot through the opening and the strap holding the waterproof sheet on him snapped. It all happened so quickly. He shot off with the sheet flying behind him and the saddlebags thumping up and down. I had visions of all the saddlebags tipping sideways, frightening him even more, but they stayed in place.

Fortunately Piglet was not in her saddlebag. The two of us ran after him then suddenly he came full gallop back towards us. I tried to stand in his way flapping my arms, but not for long. He obviously was not going to stop. By now the waterproof sheet was dragging along on the ground behind him.

Eventually, I managed to retrieve a sweating horse – packs still in place, but shaking up and down as Jester shivered with fear and gasped for breath as I managed to unfasten the waterproof sheet and told him what an idiot he was! What a waste of energy!

When we got to the end of West Drive who should we meet, but Ian Botham again, with his full entourage and various vehicles with "Ian Botham Leukaemia Walk" displayed across them and a loudspeaker announcing his coming. I soon got a collection box thrust under my nose by some enthusiastic supporter before we were allowed to continue on.

We hadn't gone many miles when I saw a car stopped ahead of us in the middle of the narrow road blocking the way. When we got to it I could see the windows were all steamed up. "Surely someone must be inside," so I knocked on a window and it opened. A woman stuck her head out and said "We've run out of petrol!"

I looked at my map. We were miles away from anywhere likely to sell petrol and so I said "I'm sorry I cannot help you" as I thought "well it's no good just sitting there waiting."

I only just managed to squeeze Jester past the car and we continued on. About a mile on down the road two cars came up behind us. I pulled Jester into the side, one car passed us but the other stopped and a man got out and came up towards me yelling "You stupid bitch, we bloody-well ran out of bloody petrol, that's why we bloody stopped, you stupid bloody cow." Then he got into his car and I thought he was going to ram into us. He was obviously aiming for us then swerved and skidded past us and was gone. "What a pleasant fellow." There must have been some stressed up atmosphere in that car – no wonder the windows were so steamed up!

We found an empty hay shed that night and I got my tent up inside it and tethered Jester so that he could graze round about and get inside the hay-shed. With all the wet weather he was relieved to get inside and lie on the old hay beside the ten. I kept hearing him come inside then a sudden thump as he lay down.

We were going along the road past Lampeter when a car passed us then stopped and a man got out and walked towards us. I wondered "what now – not more road rage I hope!" No, he was genuinely interested in what I was doing and fortunately was a local fellow and was able to tell me the route I was intending to take wasn't passable with a horse and showed me an alternative route by Llyn Brianne reservoir. It would have been very frustrating if I had gone on the way I had planned and had to turn back.

We were now starting to head east then eventually loop round and head north again.

"You'll see the 'devil's stone' on your way over the hill to the reservoir," he told me, but I couldn't see it. Maybe just as well as he explained it was where some "New Age" folks do devil worship and sacrifice animals and do some Druid rituals. Why do people want to deliberately worship the devil? They, I assume, must believe there is a devil to want to worship him. Maybe their minds are perverted by the devil himself!

It was a lovely quiet hill road through beautiful countryside on a superb sunny day. We stopped on a good grass area to have our picnic. Jester was enjoying the grass and Piglet shared my bread and cheese. I got out my camping gas stove to brew up some coffee, put my mug full of coffee down and the whole lot spilled on to the ground sheet I was sitting on and all over my trousers. Then a car stopped on the roadside near us, and a lady came across the grass towards us "May I take a photograph?" "Yes" I replied, then got up in my coffee-soaked trousers and went to get hold of Jester and called Piglet when she called out "No, I just want a picture of you."

That was a surprise. It was always Piglet and Jester people wanted a picture of, not me. Before I had time to answer her to make sure she did not want Piglet and Jester with me, she was hopping about with her camera taking pictures of me!

We were heading towards Builth Wells. I needed provisions and I also needed to draw out some money from my Post Office savings account.

When we got to Builth Wells, I tied Jester up in a yard behind the Post Office and went in with my savings book and as the cashier was seeing to me, someone in the shop called "Oh look what's coming into the shop." It was Jester with Piglet sitting in her saddlebag coming in through the open door. It caused a lot of excitement. He never liked me going out of his sight, but how had he come untied?

A lovely bridleway over the hills from Builth Wells then our last night camping in Wales on a farm near the border. Piglet and I were settled in our tent when I heard a strange crushing sound coming from the hedge next to us. What could it be? I got out of the tent to look and there was a huge bull on the other side of the hedge in the next field heaving into the hedge to look at us. Then he decided he would rub himself against it and scratch his back and the hedge was sort of crumpling up under his weight.

Suppose he comes through and decides to rub up against my tent? Piglet and I would be crushed under that weight. I stood wondering what to do. I did not want to try chasing him away in case he got annoyed. The size and weight of him; if he really wanted to push his way through that hedge I felt sure he could.

He suddenly decided he had had enough and gave me a look, then turned and slowly walked away. Suppose he came back and decided to push his way through during the night? I went back and joined Piglet in the tent and got into my sleeping bag. It was daylight next morning when I woke and no sign of the bull.

I was sad to be leaving Wales. Herefordshire seemed so busy with commuter traffic racing along its busy country roads, drivers more concerned about getting to where they were going, than what else might be on the roads. Still some lovely countryside but no bridleways going the way I wanted.

It is impossible to appreciate the countryside with traffic suddenly racing past and appearing around a bend and heading straight towards us as if we weren't there, or they had not seen us.

There was the occasional bridleway marked on my map as we got further north, but they all seemed unused and blocked with bushes and overgrown undergrowth and some even fenced off.

We were coming into Shropshire when a lady stopped her car and asked me where I had been. She said she worked for the British Horse Society teaching road safety.

I said "isn't the safest way to ride off roads?" then told her all the bridleways I had tried were unrideable. She explained she could not get any enthusiasm from local horsey people to help open the bridleways. They seemed to all have horse trailers or horse boxes to transport their horses to various horsey dos and not ride locally.

We had to skirt round Telford – all far too busy but at least the sun shone, we weren't having to cope with traffic swishing along wet roads.

Near Much Wenlock a little old lady came out of her cottage. Would I come into her cottage and join her friends having coffee? She was so excited when I said "yes;" she skipped off into the cottage to tell her friends.

I tied up Jester to her gate post and followed her in and as I got through the door was handed a glass of her home-made blackberry wine before I got my cup of coffee. I saw all her friends had an empty wine glass beside their cups of coffee. They told me she was well known for her home-made wine. It turned out a very jolly coffee party!

We camped on a farm north of Stafford near Stone overlooking the M6. I could hear the roar of traffic on it all through the night.

Next morning I went to thank the farmer for letting me camp and I remarked on the noise of the vehicles on the motorway all through the night.
"Yes" he said "it never stops, it's always busy. They want to widen it and make it into six lanes. I had to give up a lot of land when they widened it some years ago. Now they want a lot more to make it wider still. It is not going to be worth me carrying on farming if I lose any more land."

My boots were wearing out. The heels were worn right through. I knew there was a "while you wait heel bar" in Ashbourne. At least if I could get new heels on my boots, so I would not feel as if I was walking up hill all the time, I could make them do until we got home.
We got to Ashbourne and I tied Jester to a metal rail outside a building away from the busy town centre, found the heel bar and after waiting a while, walked back to Jester to find he and Piglet surrounded by a crowd of people.
Jester is always so pleased to see me return to him after he has been left for a while and he gives a loud whining. Everybody turned from looking at him and Piglet and looked at me as he gave a loud neigh when I approached and a man called out. "We thought you were at the doctors getting your feet seen to." I suddenly realised I had tied Jester to a rail leading up a ramp to a doctor's surgery. Then I remembered hearing on my pocket radio early in the morning that Fiona Campbell had completed her walk round the world but had had to have her feet injected every four hours, they had got so infected with blisters. So I called back "No, I have no blisters at all."
I kept thinking as we went through Ashbourne "soon we will be on the Tissington Trail away from all this traffic."
Next day was Sunday. I had never been on the Tissington Trail on a Sunday. It was just about as busy as the M6 – not with motor vehicles, but with bicycles. It is about sixteen miles on that old railway trail to

Buxton and as the day wore on, there were more and more cyclists speeding up behind Jester and giving him a fright: you cannot hear them coming and they kept making him jump when they suddenly appeared whooshing past us.
We left the Trail and went across towards Alstonefield and onto the old rail track up Manifold Valley instead. It was much quieter and more peaceful.

That night we camped by the river at Hume End. I kept seeing these flashes of bright blue above the water. They were kingfishers darting to and fro and diving into the river to catch fish. I spent the rest of the evening sitting watching them from my tent until it got dark. A fascinating sight.
After a few days staying with my sister on her farm, we continued on northwards. That gave me ten days to get home and get all the ponies in; their feet seen to and get them shod ready for riders to come for lessons.
October weather can be very beautiful but it can so easily give a taste of the winter ahead.
The autumn colours were spectacular as we went through the Goyt Valley and past its reservoirs. It's a very popular area for people to drive to in their cars for a day out walking, or picnicking but what is it that makes people leave their litter behind when they leave? Some had even thrown their rubbish into the reservoir which surely they must realise is water collected for human consumption. I often swear at my cows for pooing in their water trough as if I expected them to have the sense to realise they are polluting their own drinking water. I do know they are cows and have not the reasoning power to realise what they have done.
We humans do have the reasoning power to think about what the consequences can be of what we do or what we have done, but it seems as if we do not always use that power.
Is it lack of thinking beyond wanting to get rid of that rubbish and failing to think of the consequences beyond that will affect others - and even themselves?

It is like those drivers in vehicles who overtake me on Jester on a blind bend, regardless of the possibility of an unseen vehicle coming towards them and hitting them.

In both cases it is as if their immediate desire to get rid of their rubbish or to get past Jester who is holding them up, blinds them to the possible damaging consequences of their actions.

We had a cold wet and windy spell of weather when we got to the Yorkshire Dales. The daylight hours were now getting short so we did not stop for long in the middle of the day but having travelled through the area over so many years, I knew where to find good grassy and sheltered places.

One cold miserable day going to one of the places I knew; Jester remembered it as well, and was very keen to get there. We turned in off the road and oh dear, what a mess! It was only a small level area by a stream and sheltered by a wall and surrounding trees. There in the middle was a burnt area where there had been a fire and all around it was scattered rubbish.

It looked as if campers had been there and left all the rubbish in a black refuse bag which had split open and the contents scattered all over the grass.

I looked about for a clear area beyond all the empty bottles, cans, food wrappers and other discarded containers and came to a spot by the wall covered in soggy toilet paper lying on the ground. I did not look any further and dragged a reluctant Jester away thinking about the attitude of whoever had been there and left the place in such a shameful mess. Perhaps it was thoughtless youngsters, but from all the empty beer cans, drink bottles as well as the car tyre marks on the ground, I suspected whoever it was, they were not so young and they were so absorbed in their own selfish pursuit of having a good time, they were totally switched off – blind – to any thought of the shameful disregard for the countryside or anybody else wanting to enjoy it.

They had done what they wanted and left what they no longer wanted, as if their minds were not capable of stretching any further than that.

Having travelled with Sitka, my first pack pony, on journeys for fifteen years, then these seven years of journeys with Jester, I have seen a huge increase in the amount of traffic on the roads and as more and more people are driving into the countryside, I have seen how more and more areas of the countryside are getting spoilt, damaged and polluted. Narrow country roads get busier, rubbish gets chucked out from vehicles and litters the verges. Then there are the picnickers and campers who drive their vehicles onto lovely open grass areas and churn up the turf, leaving muddy tyre tracks as well as a variety of litter and rubbish.

Tractors and farm machinery have increased in size and not only do they take up the whole width of narrow roads, but being more powerful and so often driven now by a younger generation of farmers, they go along the roads at an alarming speed, often towing rattly trailers or huge modern farm implements.

I first noticed the increase in the size of tractors and farm machinery when going on journeys with Sitka into the south of England in the 1980s, where vast acreages of corn had been harvested and huge tractors were having to be used to plough up the heavy compacted soil after having the weight of all the harvesting machinery on it.

It was a time when farmers had been encouraged to progress and pull up hedges and fences to enlarge their fields and to farm more intensively to produce more. It was considered the most up to date progressive way of arable farming.

Years later it was realised that without hedges and fences as windbreaks, large amounts of top soil were being blown or washed off the land in bad weather, so farmers were encouraged to resow hedges to save losing more valuable soil.

We humans do seem bent on progressing forwards, through our continued advancement in science and technology, to having more, bigger, and better, without fully weighing up the cost of the possible side effects.

We have only to look at how species of wildlife have suffered from our progressing forward with intensive agriculture and I do wonder what damaging effects we have yet to realise from all the fungicides, pesticides we spray on our crops, often several times, over each growing season.

How much is that increase I see each year in the volume of traffic on the roads adding to polluting the air we breathe? How badly is it affecting our lungs? Then what about the side effects from all that litter and rubbish I see on the roadsides and left in the countryside that gets washed into our ditches then into streams and even into our reservoirs?

Over these years when returning home with Jester, and I have been asked "how did the journey go", I find myself saying it was very good except for the frightening way people now drive on the roads and the shocking amount of litter and rubbish I see chucked on the roadsides and in the countryside.

It leaves me thinking there seems to be something that can affect the mind and render it incapable of being able to see the damaging effects of our actions and reactions that affect our environment, our fellow being and even ourselves.

--oo--

Photo credit Helene Mauchlen

Two more books by Jane are also available from Wagtail Press

Journeys through England with a Pack Pony

Journeys through Britain with a Pack Pony 1985 – 1987

www.wagtailpress.uk